On Boxing

This book is a philosophical and cultural critique of contemporary boxing. It broadens and deepens our understanding of the empirically and normatively entwined complexities of a sport that is often misunderstood and all too easily reduced to stereotypes.

Moving between and among work in ethnography, sociology, urban studies and, especially, the philosophy of sport, and drawing on research in boxing gyms in the United States, the book presents a stereoscopic view of professional boxing as both situated cultural practice and formalized competitive sport. It takes us inside and outside the ring in discussions of the cultural embeddedness of boxing and boxing gyms, the formation of pugilistic selfhood and 'boxer cool', the nature and function of combat sport violence and sparring, and the aesthetics and ethics of cornering a boxing match. With its interdisciplinary focus on the empirical and normative dimensions of professional pugilism, *On Boxing* makes explicit the bittersweetness of the 'sweet science' and provides a new theoretical framework for analyzing boxing and, indeed, sport in general.

Written for a broad audience, this is important reading for scholars and students working in the areas of philosophy and sociology of sport and combat sport studies, as well as policymakers, coaches, and commentators engaged in the sport of boxing.

Joseph D Lewandowski is a writer, researcher, educator, and avid pugilist. A former holder of the Fulbright Masaryk Distinguished Chair in Social Studies, he currently serves as Professor of Philosophy at the University of Central Missouri, USA.

Routledge Focus on Sport, Culture and Society

Routledge Focus on Sport, Culture and Society showcases the latest cutting-edge research in the sociology of sport and exercise. Concise in form (20,000–50,000 words) and published quickly (within three months), the books in this series represents an important channel through which authors can disseminate their research swiftly and make an impact on current debates. We welcome submissions on any topic within the socio-cultural study of sport and exercise, including but not limited to subjects such as gender, race, sexuality, disability, politics, the media, social theory, Olympic Studies, and the ethics and philosophy of sport. The series aims to be theoretically-informed, empirically-grounded and international in reach, and will include a diversity of methodological approaches.

List of titles

Referees, Match Officials and Abuse
Research and Implications for Policy
Tom Webb, Mike Rayner, Jamie Cleland and Jimmy O'Gorman

Lifestyle Sports and Identities
Subcultural Careers Through the Life Course
Tyler Dupont and Becky Beal

On Boxing
Critical Interventions in the Bittersweet Science
Joseph D Lewandowski

For more information about this series, please visit: https://www.routledge.com/sport/series/RFSCS

On Boxing
Critical Interventions in the Bittersweet Science

Joseph D Lewandowski

LONDON AND NEW YORK

First published 2022
by Routledge
2 Park Square, Milton Park, Abingdon, Oxon OX14 4RN

and by Routledge
605 Third Avenue, New York, NY 10158

Routledge is an imprint of the Taylor & Francis Group, an informa business

© 2022 Joseph D Lewandowski

The right of Joseph D Lewandowski to be identified as author of this work has been asserted in accordance with sections 77 and 78 of the Copyright, Designs and Patents Act 1988.

All rights reserved. No part of this book may be reprinted or reproduced or utilised in any form or by any electronic, mechanical, or other means, now known or hereafter invented, including photocopying and recording, or in any information storage or retrieval system, without permission in writing from the publishers.

Trademark notice: Product or corporate names may be trademarks or registered trademarks, and are used only for identification and explanation without intent to infringe.

British Library Cataloguing-in-Publication Data
A catalogue record for this book is available from the British Library

Library of Congress Cataloguing-in-Publication Data
Names: Lewandowski, Joseph D., 1966- author.
Title: On boxing : critical interventions in the bittersweet science / Joseph D Lewandowski.
Description: Abingdon, Oxon ; New York, NY : Routledge, [2022] | Series: Routledge focus on sport, culture and society | Includes bibliographical references and index
Identifiers: LCCN 2021031799 | ISBN 9781032018898 (hardback) | ISBN 9781003196693 (ebook)
Classification: LCC GV1133 .L45 2022 | DDC 796.83--dc23
LC record available at https://lccn.loc.gov/2021031799

ISBN: 978-1-032-01889-8 (hbk)
ISBN: 978-1-032-05236-6 (pbk)
ISBN: 978-1-003-19669-3 (ebk)

DOI: 10.4324/9781003196693

Typeset in Times New Roman
by MPS Limited, Dehradun

For my father, a pugilist of the soul.

Contents

List of figures ix
Preface x
Acknowledgments xiii

Introduction 1

PART I
Boxing and culture 5

1 Boxing and urban culture 7
2 Pugilistic selfhood and structural violence 19
3 Boxer cool 26
4 Boxing and social capital? 33
5 The marginality of urban boxing clubs 42

PART II
Boxing and philosophy 49

6 Outline of a constraint theory of sport 51
7 Boxing as the bittersweet science of constraints 58

8 Combat sport violence and sparring 66
9 Fight plan aesthetics 75
10 Cornerman ethics 82

Conclusion 89
Index 92

Figures

1.1	West Bottoms Jalopy	8
1.2	West Bottoms Graffiti	9
1.3	Authentic Boxing Gym	9
1.4	Gym Entrance	10
1.5	Gym Car Park, 5pm	12
1.6	Happy Gilmore's Deli & Liquor	16

Preface

The 1970s was, by all accounts, one of the greatest decades in the history of heavyweight boxing in the United States. The sport was widely broadcast on network television, often eclipsed quintessentially 'American' sports, such as football and baseball, in the popular imagination, and was part of the fabric of American culture. Indeed, the boxing film *Rocky*, released in the autumn of 1976, was nominated for ten Oscar awards, won awards for Best Picture, Best Director, and Best Film Editing, and was the highest grossing film in the United States (and Canada) that year. Whether or not one liked boxing, names such as Joe Frazier, George Foreman, Ken Norton and, of course, Muhammad Ali were as familiar then as Tom Brady, Derek Jeter, and Megan Rapinoe are today.

So it was perhaps atypical but not entirely surprising that a scrawny athletic kid then growing up in a suburb of Milwaukee, Wisconsin managed to convince his father (a local Lutheran clergy) to build a makeshift boxing gym in the lower level of his family's home. A large military-style duffel bag stuffed with heavy blankets hung from the basement ceiling, a cheap speed bag poorly anchored to the wall, some gloves and a jump rope was all it took—and with that I was hooked on the sport of boxing.

Many an evening was spent hitting those bags and skipping rope, and from time to time a member of my father's local parish—Bob Inzeo: bricklayer, ex-con, and former Golden Gloves competitor—would come by to give me pointers and teach me basic combinations. This emerging interest of mine in pugilism was not confined to late night workouts in my father's homemade boxing gym, however; it spilled over into my daily life, and, indeed, even my studies at school. In response to an elementary school class assignment to write a letter to a famous person, I proudly drafted a hand-written missive to Muhammad Ali, offering a few pointers and, of all things, including an original 'float-like-a-butterfly' style poem to inspire him.

My infatuation with boxing persisted, but, with no local gym to train in, seemed destined to remain limited to bag work and those basement-training sessions with Mr. Inzeo. Until, that is, the first day of 4th grade, when a small yellow school bus rolled up to the entrance of our neighborhood school, Highland View Elementary. It must have been 1975. Under court order, Milwaukee and its surrounding all-White suburbs were in the process of desegregating their public schools. On that day 4–5 kids—Black and Brown—warily stepped out of the bus. As it turned out, two of those—Tyrone Gonzales and Lavelo McClain—were in my 4th grade class.

We quickly became friends. And in a short period of time, 'Velo'—or 'V', as everyone called him—and I became good friends. In fact, many times during the week, instead of taking the half-hour bus ride home after school, V would walk home with me and spend the afternoon and night at my house, and return to school with me the next day. We would play in the neighborhood—and we would often train and stage sparring sessions in that basement gym, bloodying one another's lip and nose from time to time in the process.

Now, this routine of having V come over after school to box went on for a while, until one day V invited me to take the yellow bus home with him and spend the weekend at *his* house. My father was against the idea, and flatly refused.

'Why?', I responded. 'Why is it ok for V to spend the night at our house but it's not ok for me to spend the night at V's house?'

My Dad looked at me and nodded, 'Ok. You can go'.

And that was that. For many weekends I went to V's house. As it happened there was a Dr. Martin Luther King, Jr. Community Center nearby. Such centers are fairly common in urban America, and are generally equipped with gymnasia, weight rooms, indoor and outdoor basketball courts, and sometimes even a pool, as well as communal rooms that can be reserved by local residents for group events. We used to spend all day on Saturday there, as the center had a boxing club of sorts. In one of the gyms volunteer coaches taught us the craft of the pugilist—how to use our hands, throw combinations, slip and counter punches, and oversaw instructive sparring matches. They also emphasized to us how to carry ourselves as boxers. They cultivated in us, that is to say, a certain sense of self: skilled but controlled; unique, but modest; confident, but respectful. We were not just kids, or 'fighters'. We were *boxers*.

Looking back now, I can say that it is thanks to those men—and Velo and that yellow bus that brought Velo to my neighborhood and me to his—that I genuinely came to know something of the sport *and culture* of boxing.

For indeed, that youthful period of friendship and pugilistic development did not take place in a socioeconomic or cultural vacuum. On the contrary, along with connecting me to a boxing club in the city, weekends at Velo's house also gave me a street-level view of human resilience and striving amid ever-diminishing opportunities and increasingly desperate material conditions. Already in the mid-1970s in Milwaukee—a longstanding industrial hub—many manufacturing and machining jobs had begun to disappear from the urban center. The demand for skilled and semi-skilled labor was declining under the pressures of neo-liberal economic policies and concomitant outsourcing of manufacturing jobs. Needless to say, this hit working class African-American communities hard. Velo's neighborhood—a place that, however ethnoracially confined and confining, once contained a functioning middle class and a variety of businesses and services—was rapidly becoming an ethnoracial trap largely devoid of businesses and services, and riddled with chronic unemployment, poverty, and criminality. In no small way the sport of boxing and the presence of boxing gyms in such communities served—and continues to serve, however precariously—as a venue of social recognition and anchors of stability.

All that is to say that, in hindsight, the first lesson I learned about the sport of boxing is that there are no easy analytic distinctions between 'inside' and 'outside' the ring or gym to be had: a philosophical treatment of the sport that uncouples it from the ways of life in which it is embedded remains at once both normatively impoverished and empirically naïve. Thus what follows is a work in the philosophy of boxing that is unavoidably also a study of boxing and culture.

Acknowledgments

I have wanted to write a book on boxing for many years. For helping me to realize that goal, I owe a debt of gratitude to a variety of individuals. Paul Gaffney, John Russell, and Jim Parry have, in crucial ways, influenced my work in the philosophy of sport. David Scott and Lynn Nead, colleagues and fellow pugilists, have informed my thinking about the links between boxing and culture. Simon Whitmore, Senior Publisher and my editor at Routledge, has provided invaluable suggestions and support at all stages of the development of this project. Martin Kreuzmann has, and continues to be, an important interlocutor on wide-ranging topics in sport, culture, and society; he is also a good friend. At the institutional level, I am especially grateful to the Czech Fulbright Commission, which supported work on this project by awarding me the Fulbright Masaryk Distinguished Chair in Social Studies; needless to say, undergraduate and graduate students in my seminars on sport and street culture at Masaryk University were the source of much insight and inspiration for this book. I have also gained much from my membership in the International Association for the Philosophy of Sport (IAPS). My family—Tina, Miles, and Sabina Lewandowski—deserve special mention for their steadfast support and sense of humor over the years; Miles was also instrumental in helping to compile the index for this book. Finally, I am grateful for the influence of my father, the Reverend Joseph M Lewandowski, who at my request as a young boy graciously agreed to construct a makeshift boxing gym in our basement on the understanding that the violent skills learned there were only to be used within the confines of the sport of boxing.

Introduction

This compact book is an interdisciplinary study in the culture and philosophy of sport, with a particular focus on urban culture and the sport of pro boxing in the United States. The overarching goal of the analysis is to develop a culturally informed philosophy of professional pugilism—to clarify and critique, that is to say, the symbolic and normative dimensions of a competitive sport that is often poorly understood in the literature and reduced to stereotypes in the popular imagination. Methodologically, the book draws on work in ethnography, sociology, urban studies and, especially, the philosophy of sport to present a stereoscopic view of boxing as both situated cultural practice and formalized competitive sport. The core methodological argument of the book is that an adequate philosophical account of boxing cannot be separated from an understanding of the sport's cultural embeddedness. That is not to say that boxing—or any sport—is reducible to culture: the chapters that follow steadfastly reject deterministic and romanticizing accounts of the sport of boxing and those individuals who opt to pursue it professionally. But neither is boxing merely a sport like many others. Indeed, the core theoretical argument of the book is that boxing is best understood as a *bittersweet* science of cultural reflexivity and rational constraints.

Such an argument is elaborated in two parts, each to be read in dialog with the other. Indeed, the purpose behind the book's organization is to establish a kind of dialogic structure in which the first part ('Boxing and Culture') provides an interactive cultural framework for the philosophical analyses developed in the second part ('Boxing and Philosophy'). Thus, Part I begins with an ethnographic look at boxing and that sport's complex relationship to certain sectors of the American urban milieu and those who inhabit it. Indeed, the role the sport of boxing and boxing gyms plays in identity and the pursuit of self-mastery—especially among individuals who are forced to endure

2 *Introduction*

various forms of physical and structural violence in America's most marginalized metropolitan districts—is the overarching subject of the first three chapters. From there the opening section shifts gears to consider the relationship between boxing and social capital, scrutinizing the extent to which participation in sport can be said to generate external goods, such as a sense of community and habits of democracy. With an eye toward further expanding and enriching the discussion of boxing and culture, the final chapter in Part I highlights the various ways in which most boxing gyms in the United States are doubly marginalized—by the twin pressures of the fitness industry and rise of Mixed Martial Arts (MMA) from the one side, and, from the other side, the relentless hollowing out of the urban life-worlds in which they remain precariously situated.

Informed by the work presented in the first half of the book, Part II seeks to develop a philosophical theory of sport that adequately captures the normative complexities of competitive boxing and, by extension, combat sport more generally. Specifically, the section begins by drawing on work by Jon Elster to outline what I call a 'constraint theory of sport'. Succinctly put, such a theory holds that engagement in competitive sport is about the interaction of choice of constraints (which game to play, as it were) and choices aimed at maximization of skill and creativity within those very constraints (how to play that game in the most excellent way possible). Yet Elster's rich thinking about rationality also includes a consideration of the ways in which such choices are themselves shaped by various given or structural constraints. Thus, a constraint theory of sport proves particularly apt in an analysis of pro boxing, as it has the distinct advantage of connecting the cultural dimensions of sport to rationality and the pursuit of excellence within sport in normatively robust and non-deterministic ways.

Indeed, a constraint theory of sport provides a critical normative tool with which to examine anew the nature and function of rules, the definition and pursuit of excellence, the relationship among violence, skills and safety, and our understanding of value, narrative, and obligations in boxing and combat sport more broadly. Hence Part II includes extended analyses of the problematic rules of boxing (as well as suggestions for their reform), an account of combat sport violence as constitutively skilled violence, and an argument for the normative potential of sparring in boxing and combat sport training more generally. The section concludes with a critical discussion of the aesthetic and ethical complexities of coaching competitive boxing. Specifically, the penultimate and closing chapters cast a critical eye on an overlooked aspect of competitive boxing—the contradictory narrative demands and moral obligations of the coach (cornerman) during the one-minute period between the rounds of a professional boxing match. Thus the study, in addition to its interdisciplinary approach, is designed to zoom in and out on various aspects of its cultural-philosophical subject matter. Chapters, and often portions within chapters, move fluidly from close-up perspectives on, for example, the inner ethnoracial dynamics of boxing gyms and the cooperative ethos of sparring to, among other things, macro-level US census data on impoverished urban neighborhoods and participation rates in fitness boxing. The argument implicit in such an approach is that it is in and through a range of perspectives—participant and observer; normative and descriptive; empirical and symbolic—that the intertwined cultural and philosophical complexities of contemporary professional boxing are best captured.

Of course 'styles make fights', as the saying goes in boxing. So, too, do they make books, especially books on boxing, a subject matter to which readers (and writers) tend to bring an exceptionally wide variety of assumptions and expectations to the conversation. In this regard, I have aimed to engage the broadest possible readership—cultural theorists and philosophers, to be sure, but also policy makers, coaches, athletes, commentators and, indeed, anyone with an interest in combat sport competition and training. Thus, I have deliberately chosen to write in a style that blends theoretical argumentation with practical examples; I have also sought to keep notes and references to a minimum. While the chapters (and sections) can be read as free-standing analyses, the book nevertheless stands as an integrated interdisciplinary mini-monograph. As such, for certain readers it inevitably will have its shortcomings—it is too interdisciplinary for some, not interdisciplinary enough for others; it omits relevant arguments and positions in one discipline or, alternatively, spends too much time on another; and so on. Be that as it may, in the end, one of the merits of an interdisciplinary book on boxing—or, indeed, any sport—lies not in its comprehensiveness but rather in its suggestiveness of further avenues of research and critique. It is my modest hope that the present study manages, however imperfectly, to accomplish precisely that.

Part I
Boxing and culture

1 Boxing and urban culture

It would not be much of an exaggeration to say that the sport of boxing is inseparable from the vicissitudes of urban life in the United States.[1] Indeed, for well over a half century, US-based boxing clubs have stood not merely as physical places typically located within the American metropolitan milieu. Rather, and more fundamentally, boxing clubs and the sport of boxing in the United States have been powerfully shaped by a distinctly urban cultural landscape—one that is often referred to as 'the ghetto' or, in the contemporary street slang of today's ghetto residents, 'the hood'.

Thus, it is the intersection of boxing and urban life that I want to characterize in detail here as a way to begin to establish the cultural framework for the arguments to be presented in this book.[2] More specifically, in this chapter I shall draw on several years of experience as an active member of a locally owned Kansas City boxing gym to describe some of the complex ways in which various structures and forces of life in 'the hood' shape the agency and conception of selfhood of many athletes who opt to pursue the sport of boxing in the United States.[3] The point of such a description is not to romanticize or aestheticize boxing or, for that matter, American urban life; there are few 'rags-to-riches' narratives to be found in a typical urban American boxing gym. Still less, however, do I want to reduce boxers deterministically to so many effects of the empirical and historical forces of their urban contexts.[4] Instead, the primary aim here is to begin to open a critical window into the demimonde of the professional pugilist.

In Kansas City, as in many urban gyms in the United States, most professional boxers labor in obscurity, only to realize modest, if any, success in the sport. Indeed, the relative obscurity of boxers from places like Kansas City is perhaps surpassed only by the shabby and faceless gyms in which they train. While its neighbor to the east, Detroit, boasts the Kronk Boxing Gym; and Brooklyn has Gleason's and LA has the Wild Card; Kansas City is home to boxers and boxing gyms whose names few outside of the city have ever heard—gyms like Eastside, the Whatsoever Boxing Club, and my former gym, Authentic Boxing.

It was on a scorching July afternoon that I finally managed, after three unsuccessful attempts, to find the gym. Established in 1998, the gym lies just outside the shadows of the 12th Street Bridge and is housed in the basement of one of the many mostly abandoned ware- and packinghouses in the 19th century industrial district of Kansas City known as the 'West Bottoms'.

Today, the area remains largely a kind of no-man's-land; an artifact of a bygone era in the city's history where few people actually reside, but where a set of distinctly urban structures and agents converge in various ways.[5] In fact, the West Bottoms functions, like many such places, as point of intersection and magnet for a variety of urban practices, social interactions, and commerce, not only boxing but also street-walking (low-income and high-risk prostitution), drug-dealing, street-peddling, evangelizing, scavenging, pay day loan centers and check-cashing services, among others (Figures 1.1 and 1.2).

I found the gym with the help of a man who, along with two dogs, was scavenging for food and aluminum cans in a dumpster nearby.

'Hey, excuse me, can you tell me where the Authentic Boxing club is?', I inquired.

Figure 1.1 West Bottoms Jalopy. Photograph by the author.

Figure 1.2 West Bottoms Graffiti. Photograph by the author.

Figure 1.3 Authentic Boxing Gym. Photograph by the author.

'Man, you standin' right in front of the muthafucka', he answered as he looked up, witheringly, through the late afternoon haze of heat.

'That?', I said, gesturing toward the two-story shell of brick in front of me (Figure 1.3).

He nodded. The old warehouse seemed both threatened and threatening. Years of neglect had given it the appearance of being

Figure 1.4 Gym Entrance. Photograph by the author.

dangerously close to collapsing under its own weight, and this precariousness in turn gave the building the general feel of a place better left unentered.

The few windows on the first floor were heavily boarded, the gravel lot that surrounded the building was strewn with trash and more than one stripped and burned-out car. One side of the building had no windows at all—only a heavy metal door punctuated the brick (Figure 1.4).

As I opened the door that day the smell and the heat were stifling. Bud-dum, bud-dum, bud-dum, ding-ding-ding—the sounds of the bags and timing bell mixed with the beats of a thumping boom box. But no gym or fighters were to be seen from the point of entry. To my right was a downward facing staircase. From the top of the stairs all that could be seen was a cracked old school landline telephone dangling from the wall at the base of the stairway.

I hesitated and resolved to leave. But just then the phone rang, and a tall guy with a silvery ponytail moved into my field of vision at the base of the stairs to answer it. As he did so, he spotted me and gestured for me to come down.

Slowly I made my way down the stairs. By the time I reached the bottom he had hung up the phone.

'You new?', he asked.

'Uhm, yes', I stammered, peering around the corner and catching my first glimpse of the gym interior.

'Yo, we got a live one up in here', he yelled, to no one in particular.

'You livin' in the mission over there?', he asked.[6]

'Uhm, no, I have my own place', I answered, not anticipating the question.

'I'm Monty. Coach ain't here today. Come back tomorrow. Gym hours is Mondays through Thursdays, 5 to 8, Fridays till 7'.

Returning the next day, I meet Coach Edgar. He takes me into his ramshackle office. In a few fumbling sentences, I tell him that I used to box as an amateur, when I was a kid back in Milwaukee. But it has been many many years since I have been in the ring. I say that I want to train, get in shape, work on my skills, be a good sparring partner for his guys—in boxing parlance, I offer myself as a 'gym fighter'.

'What about you?', he asks. 'This ain't no health club. This gym takes and gives', he says. 'Everyone sweats the same sweat down here. You thinking pro or amateur? Judging by your age, pro would be better for you. Might as well get paid. N' I can control who you fight, set up a couple of smokers for you.[7] It's a lotta' guys will fight just to make some money. You think about what you want from the gym'.

'Ok', I say.

Feeling as if I am in over my head, I redirect the conversation.

'So, are there any fees or membership dues or anything'?

'Nope', Coach Edgar answers, 'no fees, but it ain't free, either; you pay in blood and sweat down here'.

He sells me a pair of handwraps, and I agree to start the next day.

Weeks go by. With no air conditioning or fans, the gym is so goddamned hot that I come near to fainting during the first weeks. But, eventually, the work starts to feel good, and in another month or so I begin to reclaim some of my skills. The humidity and the smell and the roaches, the music, the sound of the bags and the bell—all these start to become familiar to me (Figure 1.5).

The gym is ethnoracially diverse. Most of the boxers are Black, with the rest evenly split between Mexican and White. Later I learn that most of the Black boxers live east of Troost Avenue, in an historically

12 *Boxing and culture*

Figure 1.5 Gym Car Park, 5pm.

Black district of the city that continues to serve as a locus of ethnoracial division and enclosure; while most of the Mexican and White boxers reside either in an area known as 'Northeast' or in Kansas City, Kansas, both ethnoracially mixed and largely impoverished and crime ridden parts of Kansas City's urban core.

In conversations overheard, I glean that the types of employment among the boxers varies within a fairly narrow range of skilled, semi-skilled, and low-level service industry jobs: welder, mason, painter, drywaller, roofer, airport baggage handler, FedEx warehouse package handler—several of the guys work at the local FedEx facility—and, of course, a handful of fast-food workers. A few of them also work, occasionally, as bouncers or doormen at local nightclubs.

New guys show up all the time—adorned with baseball caps on sideways, bandanas tied on their heads, gold chains around their necks, and other 'hood'-inflected accouterment.

In the course of weeks, I come to observe a kind of ritual that repeats itself as gym prospects arrive in this way for the first time. Descending the stairs, Coach Edgar catches sight of them and never fails to yell out: 'Yo, get that shit off your head. This ain't no ghetto up in here'!

The new guys oblige. Some last, but most are gone in a week or two. The reflexive adaptation of the world of the 'hood' to the world of the gym is simply more than most can manage.[8]

Aside from Coach Edgar, no one really talks to me, and for a long while I endure a kind of social invisibility.

Then one day later that summer one of the guys turns toward me during the one-minute interval between rounds on the speed bag and asks:

'How long you been boxin'?

'I used to box as a kid, but it's been over 20 years', I answer.

'Damn, that long?'. He pauses, puzzled, and then asks: 'You been in the joint?'[9]

'No, nothing like that', I say.

'They call me Little Mike', he says.

'I'm Joseph', I answer. The bell rings, and we go back to the bags.

With that exchange Mike and I begin to talk on occasion. And I gradually become visible to the other guys in the gym; in the months that follow I get to know most of the boxers.

There's Coach Edgar's son, Rocky (his real name). In his mid-twenties, Rocky has already fought repeatedly in the local professional scene. And he has the short-term memory loss to prove it. Once, when I asked him where his upcoming fight was to be held, he responded, 'Shit, bro, I don't even know. When you take punches fo' a living you gotta' be somewhere three o' fo' times fo' you remember it'.

Then there's Dennis, 'The Punisher'. An ultra-lean welterweight, also in his mid-twenties, Dennis is the best pound-for-pound male boxer in the gym, and eventually ends up moving to Las Vegas to train. In our squalid locker room, there is a poster with an image of Dennis alongside Muhammad Ali. The caption reads: 'He was just another skinny Black kid once, too'. I never found out who made that poster, but I always liked it. Needless to say, so did Dennis.

There is John, 'The Terminator' and Big Will, both big heavyweights; Jesse, 'The Mexican Assassin', Rafael, Maurice, Little Maurice (Maurice's son), Little John, Ernest, Bud, 'Pretty Boy' Keith; and Greg, my frequent sparring partner. In a heated spar later that autumn, Greg badly bruises my ribs. I take some time off from the gym to recover, only to find out later through a chance encounter on my university campus that Greg is in fact a student at my university.

I also get to know Aaron (nicknamed 'The Blaxican'), a decent welterweight who later that year ends up fighting Julio Cesar Chavez, Jr.

in Madison Square Garden. Aaron got TKO'd in the third round, but he never stopped talking about that trip to New York.

And, in time, I get acquainted with the best female boxer in the gym, Franchesca, known as 'The Chosen One'. While professional club fighters in places like Kansas City typically earn paltry sums, with up to 40% of the total purse going to their coach/trainer and promoter, Franchesca proves to be the exception.[10] She is in fact one of the best fighters—male or female—at Authentic, and eventually goes on to become a world-ranked contender, competing for titles in bouts held in Canada, Germany, and the United States.

Franchesca, like many other professional female (and male) boxers, moves in and out of other forms of combat sport competition, such as MMA, and other bodily crafts, especially modeling of various kinds.[11] As it happens, she is a former three-time Ms. Hawaiian Tropic US finalist and Miss January Ringside calendar girl. At the professional level, the sport of boxing embraces this kind of hypersexualization of women—regardless of their talent in the ring—and then eagerly commodifies the sexualized female pugilist to promote and sell fights. Franchesca's first live televised professional fight is an ESPN Friday Night Fights pay-per-view affair held at the Playboy Mansion in Los Angeles against none other than a former Playboy cover girl.

Yet Franchesca is also featured in a series of seven prominent no frills instructional boxing videos with the legendary trainer, Freddie Roach. Filmed in the Wild Card gym, the videos contain no trace of the kind of reifying sexualization used to promote her high-profile fights, and are still in use today. Indeed, the 'beauty queen turned boxer' trope may hype fights, but in the lived space of a working boxing gym and practiced craft of a professional female boxer it is nowhere to be found. On the contrary, it is clear that 'The Chosen One' is *a boxer*—one of the best pure boxers at Authentic—who, despite her pugilistic pedigree, trains alongside, spars with, and supports even the most modestly skilled women and men in the gym.

As time passes, I also come to know the other players in the gym: Frank, one of the coach's assistants; Monty, the tall pony-tailed guy who, as it turns out, owns the warehouse and several others in the area and is the gym's promoter. The gym's financial structure is convoluted and fragile. I learn from Rocky and some of the other guys that Monty's other warehouses are elaborately outfitted as haunted houses, complete with permanent installations, live actors, and interactive tours. With names like 'The Edge of Hell' and 'The Beast', the haunted houses are legendary among local Kansas City youths. The houses open in late September, and operate the entire month of October, when they charge entry fees starting at $25. Monty hires some of the boxers, including Rocky, to work in the houses, take tickets, do crowd control, and so on. From what I can glean, the money Monty makes on the haunted houses helps to subsidize the gym. All the guys hate Monty, whom they refer to as a 'lil' bitch' for the ways he pressures them to take fights on short notice, and to work extra hours in the haunted houses every autumn.

I come to recognize a kaleidoscope of others—wives, girlfriends, brothers, sisters, lots of young kids and babies, and various associates who come and go and often sit on the four or five beat up plastic chairs that line the exterior wall of Coach Edgar's office. The cast of characters varies greatly from day to day. On some days I see nothing but familiar faces. On other days, especially Fridays, of the people training, only Rocky, Dennis and Aaron are familiar to me.

Along with Rocky, Denis and Aaron, the boxer I get to know fairly well is Erik—a cruiserweight with a 2–3 record, originally from Gary, Indiana. Erik and I typically arrive to the gym early. Sometimes I see him sitting around the corner, leaning up against the side of the building, smoking weed. We talk a lot. Well, actually, Erik talks and I listen. Like me, he trains long and hard, and is a regular at the gym. But he's not much of a boxer—or athlete, for that matter. I saw him fight once. After a poor showing in the first round, Erik got himself disqualified in the second round when he grabbed his counterpart and threw him, wrestling style, to the mat.

One late August afternoon Erik and I were waiting for coach Edgar to open up the gym. Coach wasn't late. We were early once again. And Erik was talking about the 'shit' he had to deal with living with all those other 'homeless mutha fuckahs', as he put it, in the mission.

A prostitute walked by, slowly, on her way to Happy Gilmore's, the check-cashing, deli and liquor cornerstore nearby, where the daily lifeworld of 'the hood' was always in full effect (Figure 1.6).

As she passed by Erik shook his head, turned to me and said:

> Man, I know I ain't all that either, you know. But its two ways of doin' things—with style, and without. Everybody recognize style...and I got plenty a' that. It's all about style, bro, it's all about style...

A few months later Erik is gone. When I ask Rocky what happened, he says, simply, 'My Pops got sick of his ass'. Someone said later that Erik wound up in East LA. I never heard from him again.

16 *Boxing and culture*

Figure 1.6 Happy Gilmore's Deli & Liquor. Photograph by the author.

Among the many conversations and characters I experienced at Authentic Boxing, Erik's introspective comments about 'style' and that poster of Denis and Muhammad Ali have always stuck with me. Culturally, to be sure, the boxing gym 'ain't no ghetto', as Coach Edgar ritualistically insisted. But it is a site for the cultivation of a certain kind of self *from within* the 'hood'. Indeed, there is a profound tension between, on the one hand, the way in which so many boxers from mediocre fight towns like Kansas City are used, prostitute-like, as fodder in the sport of boxing and, on the other hand, those boxers' own reflexive attempts to assert their agency and articulate a unique kind of self from within the confines of their local urban milieu. In boxing, the construction of identity (culture) and the pursuit of excellence (sport) intersect in unexpected ways. For one may not be much of a competitive athlete, one may be 'ghetto', one may even be homeless—but all that looks different when one is *a boxer*.

In the years at Authentic, that is to say, I came to understand—once again, after so much time away from the sport—that becoming a boxer is as much a *cultural* as it is an athletic achievement. Indeed, one of the central lessons to be gleaned from the gym is that mere dedication to the sport of boxing plays a decisive role in the construction of a distinct selfhood that is valued as much, if not more, than the realization of athletic excellence in competition. Paradoxically, at the cultural level just *being a boxer*—striving to achieve what I shall characterize in the next chapter as a 'pugilistic selfhood'—in difficult urban contexts means more than being a good boxer. In boxing, the sheer cultural value of sport can and often does outweigh the athletic value of excellence.

Notes

1 Of course, I do not pretend to be the first to make such a connection. For perhaps the best single study of the 'urban geography' of boxing, see Heiskanen (2012).
2 For related and insightful book-length studies of boxing, see Boddy (2008), Scott (2009), Wacquant (2003), Rotella (2003), and Trimbur (2013). For an influential literary take on pugilism, one needs look no further than Oates (2009); and for an important extension of Oates' work, see Woodward (2012). For a more recent and powerful literary exploration of the intersection of boxing and race in the US context, see especially Albertyn (2019). The present study departs from the aforementioned works inasmuch as it attempts to make explicit *both* the cultural *and* philosophical dimensions of boxing.
3 For a more in-depth and properly ethnographic look at boxing and urban culture, see especially the earlier work of Wacquant (1992, 1995).
4 Thus, mistakenly seeking to explain the cultural and philosophical dimensions of the sport of boxing by looking simply 'outside the ring', as it were.
5 Though even here signs of processes of gentrification have become evident, as local artists and others have begun to occupy and convert many warehouses into loft-style studios and places of business—a development we shall consider briefly in chapter 5.
6 The reference is to the City Union Mission, a nearby homeless shelter founded by local ministers in 1924.
7 A 'smoker' is an unsanctioned full contact fight with a referee and judges of some sort but no professional medical staff. Designed to help boxers hone their skills in competition, smokers do not become part of a boxer's win–loss record. They are, in essence, illegal contests that occupy a gray zone between sparring and an actual match.
8 An analysis of this process is one of the central concerns of the ensuing two chapters.
9 In this context 'joint' is slang for jail.

10 The purses for professional boxers vary greatly by geography and level of competition. And like many low-level laborers, boxers tend to exaggerate their earnings. But in places like Kansas City, $100-$200USD per round for entry-level pro fighters with no pedigree is not uncommon.
11 For two helpful discussions of women's boxing, see Smith (2014) and Rotella (1999).

References

Albertyn, David. 2019. *Undercard*. Toronto: House of Anansi Press.
Boddy, Kasia. 2008. *Boxing: A Cultural History*. London: Reaktion Books.
Heiskanen, Benita. 2012. *The Urban Geography of Boxing: Race, Class, and Gender in the Ring*. New York: Routledge.
Oates, Joyce. 2009. *On Boxing*. New York: Harper.
Rotella, Carlo. 1999. 'Good with Her Hands: Women, Boxing, and Work.' *Critical Inquiry* 25 (3): 566–598.
Rotella, Carlo. 2003. *Cut Time: An Education at the Fights*. New York: Houghton Mifflin.
Scott, David. 2009. *The Art and Aesthetics of Boxing*. Lincoln, NE: University of Nebraska Press.
Smith, Malissa. 2014. *A History of Women's Boxing*. Lanham, MD: Rowman and Littlefield.
Trimbur, Lucia. 2013. *Come Out Swinging: The Changing World of Boxing in Gleason's Gym*. Princeton, NJ: Princeton University Press.
Wacquant, Loic. 1992. 'The Social Logic of Boxing in Black Chicago: Towards a Sociology of Pugilism.' *Sociology of Sport Journal* 9 (3): 221–254.
Wacquant, Loic. 1995. 'The Pugilistic Point of View: How Boxers Think and Feel about Their Trade.' *Theory and Society* 24 (4): 489–535.
Wacquant, Loic. 2003. *Body and Soul*. Oxford: Oxford University Press.
Woodward, Kath. 2012. 'The Culture of Boxing: Sensation and Affect.' *Sport in History* 31 (4): 487–503.

2 Pugilistic selfhood and structural violence

While Erik was a particularly hard case, it would not be an understatement to say that, from the standpoint of the *sport* of professional boxing, the boxers at Authentic were nothing special. With the notable exception of Franchesca, none of them went anywhere with their careers, they all earned precious little money, most were of modest athletic abilities, and only a few managed winning records. It thus became apparent to me that the gap between the sheer banality of their skill levels and circumstances, and their distinctive self-understanding and identification *as boxers*, could only be adequately understood in cultural terms. For indeed, despite their subpar win-loss records, miniscule earnings, and a professional career that consigned them to fodder within the wider world of pro boxing, the men and women at Authentic articulated and exuded a unique sense of self. In a context where 'everybody recognize style', to borrow Erik's phrase, the sport of boxing and distinction of being a boxer were in themselves expressions of autonomy and an achievement of a kind of identity *worth recognizing*.[1] Regardless of one's record, skills, or earnings, simply being a boxer was in their world already a valued mark of distinction and successful striving. Being a boxer made one something more than another marginal inhabitant of 'the hood' or 'just another skinny black kid'.

What I came to observe, I want to argue here, was the striving to achieve a kind of pugilistic selfhood—a unique fashioning of the self that was neither entirely separable from nor easily reduced to the urban milieu in which so much about the sport of boxing is entwined. Culturally speaking, to be a boxer in such places is to engage in a reflexive mode of recognizing and being recognized within a milieu of profound scarcity, violence, and disrespect. In this regard, the sport of boxing intersects with culture in ways rather different than one finds in most other sports. When viewed from the ground up, as it were, we see that in boxing, unlike in, say, badminton or bowling or baseball, individuals actively strive to negotiate and transform *themselves and their relation to the difficult world in which they are situated*.[2]

This striving to achieve such a reflexive agency is remarkable, especially when one realizes that most American boxers reside in those sectors of US cities where the state—and the market—have largely retreated and where physical violence and bodily insecurity are part of everyday existence. In fact, deprivation, disrespect and, especially, physical violence pervade and largely come to define daily life in such places. The forms of physical violence endemic to such spaces are all too familiar and range from episodic street corner disputes regarding perceived displays of disrespect to drug-trade-related clashes over territorial control and more orchestrated gang-related retaliations. In these and countless other moments, an individual's familiarity with and capacity to assert (or withhold) physical violence at the right times and in the right ways is crucial to getting on with everyday life.

Yet participation in the sport of boxing is not merely about individuals' or groups' relationship to daily physical violence. This is a common misconception in work on boxing and combat sport more generally. Arguments that reduce participation in pugilism to mere preferences or tendencies of violent individuals or stereotypical notions about 'cultures of violence' should be steadfastly rejected. Boxers are no more—and no less—inherently violent than other athletes, though as noted above, because of their life circumstances they typically have a deep familiarity with fear and physical violence.[3]

While physical violence is for the most part visible and transpires in the foreground of daily life in many metropolitan settings, there is another, more formative, kind of violence typically at work in the everyday world of the pugilist—one characteristically ignored in studies of sport violence—namely, '*structural violence*'.[4] Both in terms of its functions and its effects, structural violence must be distinguished from the problematic notion of 'cultures of violence'. An account of structural violence is, or so I want to maintain here, crucial to clarifying the layers of violence present in the sport of boxing (at least in the US context); it is also essential to explain the attraction of pugilistic selfhood for those routinely exposed to such violence.

Structural violence is tacit, indirect, and seemingly agentless. In the face of structural violence, individuals typically feel and yet often struggle to make explicit and grasp the complex functioning and corrosive effects of such an elusive force on their minds and bodies and ways of life. Most generally, structural violence amounts to the more or less hidden ways in which macro-level forces constrain individuals in ways that place them at risk—or exacerbate existing risks—for physical, economic, social, and psychic harm. Or, to put the matter in Paul Farmer's terms:

> Structural violence is violence exerted systematically ... hence the discomfort these ideas provoke in a moral economy still geared to pinning praise or blame on individual actors. ... the concept of structural violence is intended to inform the study of the social machinery of oppression. (Farmer 2004, 307)

Structural violence is thus a particularly insidious structured and structuring mechanism of oppression that engenders human depredation and suffering. Structural violence not only limits what can be thought and/or done. More fundamentally, structural violence's diffusive power and refractive effects make it exceptionally difficult for individuals caught within it to see it and bring it into focus. In this way, structural violence not only damages agents but also tends to hinder their power to scrutinize and articulate the causes and effects of that damage. In his medical anthropological study of Haiti, Farmer describes the link between human suffering and structural violence in the following way:

> ... such suffering is 'structured' by historically given (and often economically driven) processes and forces that conspire—whether through routine, or, as is more commonly the case, the hard surfaces of life—to constrain agency ... While certain kinds of suffering are readily observable ... structural violence all too often defeats those who would describe it. (Farmer 2003, 40)

Now, admittedly, Kansas City is not Port-au-Prince. Yet many of its local boxers are routinely subjected to structural violence through systemic racism and neoliberalism. In fact, these two interconnected forms of structural violence must be highlighted here for the ways in which they continue to constrain agency and shape the 'hard surfaces' of the daily lives of those individuals most likely to train in places like Authentic Boxing.

In the first instance, the principles of division and enclosure that inform the history of US cities have proven to be an unexpectedly durable form of structural violence. 'Dark' and 'Brown' ghettos, like the one east of Troost Avenue in Kansas City, persist as the locus of entrapment for many ethnoracial subgroups. In fact, in the built environments of what were once 'institutional ghettos'—sites of ethnoracial enclosure where residents nevertheless managed to exert a certain measure of social stability, control, and neighborhood organization—one finds today, amid the striking ruins and decay of once architecturally significant neighborhoods, profound anomie, isolation, and crushing poverty.[5] With poorly lit streets, a dearth of public transportation, health, grocery and commercial services, and abandoned lots and boarded up houses, these 'new American ghettos' coalesce to do violence to the hearts and minds and dreams of those subject to them, and bear witness to the degeneration of what were once functioning urban *neighborhoods* to '*the hood*'.[6]

In the second instance, along with the structural violence of processes of ghettoization, any consideration of boxing and culture must also highlight the more recent ravaging effects of the storm of neoliberalism and concomitant 'globalization-friendly' policy shifts that have disemboweled the manufacturing economies upon which so many urban working-class dwellers once depended for their livelihood, community stability, and economic dignity. 'Institutional ghettos' have thus become 'jobless ghettos'.[7] In this way, the 'hard surfaces' of the ethnoracialized 'hood' have been made infinitely sharper and harder by the economic forces of neoliberalism in US urban policy-making. While the proletarian sport of boxing very much reflects working-class life as a physical vocation and bodily craft, the structural violence wrought by economic globalization has largely undermined working-class existence in such places.

What makes structural violence so insidious is not merely its effects, but how it comes to operate, subcutaneously, as it were, in the minds and bodies of individuals. Infection-like, the effects of structural violence course through the very being of individual agents and exert themselves continually. Individuals don't merely reside 'in the hood'; rather, in time 'the hood' comes to live '*in*' them, as the saying goes. The pernicious effects of structural violence—of lives lived in and damaged by such durable and demeaning mechanisms of oppression—defeats many of 'those who would describe it', as Farmer suggests.

Given the prevalence of structural violence in America's 'new' ghettos, one might be tempted to think that such violence generates precisely the kind of disrespected and self-disrespecting individuals most likely to offer themselves up, unwittingly, as fodder in the sport of pro boxing. Yet in the context of a culturally informed discussion of the pursuit of pugilistic selfhood, I would argue the opposite. Indeed, the notion that structural violence operates behind the backs—or over the heads—of boxers who live in 'the hood' is in my experience profoundly paternalistic. The demimonde of the pugilist is rich with critical insights into the structural violence unique to 'the new American ghetto'.

Indeed, a palpable vibe of structural violence hung in the sweat-filled air of Authentic Boxing, and often reverberated, literally, throughout the gym, thanks to that old boom box, which played songs about 'the hood' and the pervasiveness of such violence. During that time hip hop music continued its prominence, and I recall frequently hearing Kanye West's 'All Falls Down' (2004) while I trained. Among other things, the song's lyrics contain a critique of what living the 'American dream' of upward mobility in fact means for folks with Black and Brown skin. In particular, the song makes explicit the extent to which, despite having achieved the outward trappings of material success, a Black man in a Mercedes Benz is still just an 'N-word' in a coupe.

Such tracks were as much a part of the gym as the bags, ring, and round timer were, and expressed a reflexive understanding of the painful limits of a daily life oppressed and disrespected by the structural violence of racism and neoliberalism.

Thus, while there are perhaps myriad ways to explain how and why an individual chooses to participate in the sport of boxing, attributing that decision to 'cultures of violence' or even an individual appetite for physical violence is reductive. Put simply: the argument here is that the pursuit of pugilistic selfhood is a *critical* response to the painful constraints of *structural violence*. In taking up the sport of boxing individuals fashion a different kind of self vis-à-vis others and their world.[8] Indeed, in voluntarily submitting themselves to the arduous rigors and limits of the gym—in adhering to Coach Edgar's ritualistic admonishment that the gym 'ain't no ghetto'—individuals choose to limit their own agency in ways that create new value, status, and respect for their sense of self.

Here we see precisely how and why, from a cultural vantage point, the achievement of becoming a boxer is tied not so much to athleticism or competitive success but rather to the steadfast dedication to a wide and seemingly endless variety of *self*-impositions. Committing to the daily training regimes of the sport, accepting taboos on street-fighting, practicing dietary restrictions, limiting sexual activities during training camps, continually working to master individual responses to pain, fear, and the threat of harm in the ring—in these, and countless other self-imposed ways, boxers assert the kind of relative autonomy vis-à-vis constraints that is characteristically put out of reach by oppressive mechanisms of structural violence.[9]

In boxing, that is to say, victims of structural violence manage to wrestle a realm of freedom, however limited, from a realm of painful necessity. Electing to adhere to the constraints of boxing—stepping into the gym and ring and becoming *a boxer*—lends form and content to a unique identity that distinguishes an individual from others within the urban milieu. Put differently, the *cultural sweetness* of the sweet science of boxing lies in how the elective adoption of its constraints enables the reflexive accomplishment and recognition of a form of agency and identity all too scarcely realized in 'the hood'.

In sum, in thinking about what moves individuals in many urban contexts to become boxers, an adequate understanding of structural violence is key. In boxing, individual agents take up a highly reflexive relationship to the durable but elusive mechanisms of oppression tacitly imposed by the force of structural violence in their own urban milieu and opt to pursue a different path in constituting their identities. Qua boxers, individuals commit themselves to a unique self-fashioning in a world where the structural conditions of possibility of such a presentation are painfully limited. Of course, the achievement of pugilistic selfhood does not, prima facie, allow boxers to escape 'the hood'; autonomy is always relative autonomy. Nor does it necessarily make them excellent boxers. But it does lend them a distinctive kind of status and recognition—a 'style' everybody recognizes, as Erik remarked—in a world riddled with structural violence.

Notes

1 Drawing on work in recognition theory, and focusing on selfhood and self-love, Anderson (2021) has recently sought to develop precisely this point in the context of work in the philosophy of sport.
2 Wacquant (1995) makes a similar point when he suggests that '... boxers decisively realign the structure and texture of their entire existence—its temporal flow, its cognitive and sentient profile, its psychological and social complexion—in ways that put them in a unique position to assert their agency' (510).
3 A topic to be addressed at length in the next chapter.
4 The concept appears first in Galtung and Hoivik (1971) but is developed more fully in Farmer (2003, 2004).
5 The history and functions of 'institutional ghettos' are explored in detail by Wilson (1997).
6 For a powerful photo-ethnography of the rise of 'new American ghettos', see Vergara (1995).
7 The discussion of the transformation of 'institutional ghettos' to 'jobless' ones is the specific focus of Wilson (1997), and crucial to an understanding of the demise of many urban boxing clubs, as we shall see in chapter 5.
8 Of course boxing is also a profoundly working-class endeavor, as Wacquant (1995, 2003) has argued and as we have already noted here. Pro boxers understand and typically characterize their craft as 'work', a 'job', a 'living'

and so on. Boxing is surely a working-class sport, and, like many professional combat sports, can serve as a way to augment incomes from other sources. But with such modest sums at stake in most competitions, and in light of the danger and physical toll of boxing, the value of the sport cannot be adequately measured solely in economic terms.

9 On this point see also Wacquant (1995), who alludes to the appeal of the enabling constraints of boxing when he says that 'for boxers, it [prizefighting] represents the potential means for carving out a margin of autonomy from their oppressive circumstances and for expressing their ability to seize their own fate and remake it in accordance with their inner wishes' (501).

References

Anderson, Wivi. 2021. 'Sport and Self-Love: Reflections on Boxing and the Construction of Selfhood.' *Journal of the Philosophy of Sport* 48 (1): 129–145.

Farmer, Paul. 2003. *Pathologies of Power: Health, Human Rights, and the New War on the Poor*. Berkeley, CA: University of California Press.

Farmer, Paul. 2004. 'An Anthropology of Structural Violence.' *Current Anthropology* 45 (3): 305–325.

Galtung, Johan, and Tord Hoivik. 1971. 'Structural and Direct Violence: A Note on Operationalization.' *Journal of Peace Research* 8 (1): 73–76.

Vergara, Camilo. 1995. *The New American Ghetto*. Rutgers, NJ: Rutgers University Press.

Wacquant, Loic. 1995. 'The Pugilistic Point of View: How Boxers Think and Feel about Their Trade.' *Theory and Society* 24 (4): 489–535.

Wacquant, Loic. 2003. *Body and Soul*. Oxford: Oxford University Press.

West, Kayne. 2004. 'All Falls Down.' *College Dropout*. Def Jam Recordings and Roc-A-Fella Records.

Wilson, William Julius. 1997. *When Work Disappears: The World of the New Urban Poor*. New York: Random House.

3 Boxer cool

Many athletes strategically adopt a deliberate 'look'—a 'game face', in sport parlance—for the purpose of gaining an edge in competition. Indeed, individual athletes in many sports often intentionally 'stare down' opponents, or, conversely, seek to appear carefree, even smiling at an opponent. Others still may opt to exhibit a genuinely emotionless 'poker face', in the hope of masking their emotional states and intentions in pursuit of victory. Such deliberate and outward non-verbal bodily strategies of intimidation, misdirection, and masking are a familiar component of many sport competitions, and can play a role, however difficult to ascertain precisely, in winning or losing. Boxers, of course, also engage in embodied attempts to intimidate, misdirect, and mask in the heat of competition. Perhaps one of the most familiar of these is when, in the course of a bout, a boxer is hit cleanly with a crisp blow to the head and responds with a look of nonchalance—casually dropping his guard and shrugging his shoulders as if to say, 'That all you got?'.

In the literature devoted to the philosophy of sport, this kind of comportment is often theorized via an account of 'gamesmanship' (Howe 2004; Leota and Turp 2020). But in a boxer's comportment vis-à-vis violence there is much more at work than merely a strategic-rational conception of 'gamesmanship'. In fact, uniquely in boxing (and perhaps other combat sports) this look of pugilistic nonchalance is not merely the deployment of a momentary or intentional individual strategy—as it is in, say, the 'stare down' a pitcher engages in with a home-run hitter in baseball. It is, more fundamentally, the manifestation and reflexive adaptation of a culturally inflected pose of undaunted self-mastery in the face of danger.[1] The pitcher's demeanor is clearly individual and strategic, the boxer's is far more cultural and dispositional. Gamesmanship is, as the term implies, a *game day* rational strategy; pugilistic nonchalance is an extension of a cultural

DOI: 10.4324/9781003196693-3

repertoire of orientations vis-à-vis violence. In fact, pugilistic nonchalance—or 'boxer cool', as I want to characterize it in this chapter—is never individually reducible to an episodic game day (or 'fight night') strategy. Rather, boxer cool is best understood as an athletic extension of a culturally informed and ingrained stance toward the physical and emotional threat or presence of harm.

Put differently, there is a kind of navigational know-how vis-à-vis violence (physical and structural)—a *cultural epistemology of cool*—at work in the practiced air of pugilistic nonchalance. In what follows, I want to amplify key aspects of boxer cool in an effort to capture yet another cultural dimension operative in becoming a boxer. The discussion of boxer cool should also go some way to explaining how and why, as I observed throughout my years in the gym, many individuals who undertake the sport of boxing are, modest athletic abilities aside, somehow willing and able to persist undauntedly in the sport for years.

With the exception of Ralph Wiley's boxing memoir (1989), the nature and function of pugilistic nonchalance has largely escaped observation in the study of the sport of boxing. Yet even in Wiley's discussion, boxer cool—or 'serenity', as he puts it—gets short shrift. Indeed, the notion of 'serenity' serves as the title and organizing principle of the book, but the concept itself remains dormant and merely metaphorical, inadequately attributed either to boxers' life-and-death experiences in the ring or to repeatedly concussive head trauma that undermines their cognitive ability to gauge danger sufficiently. He suggests that serenity is a state of being possessed by those who 'understand the futilities of worries and strife', and that boxers possess serenity 'to a greater degree than ordinary people' (Wiley 1989, 1). Understood this way, the term is inapt: serenity implies a kind of peacefulness and state of being at one with the world that is surely the opposite of pugilistic selfhood, which, as we have seen, demands daily striving, resilience, and self-imposed constraints in contexts of physical and structural violence and strife. Pace Wiley, boxers may exhibit many dispositions, but serenity is almost certainly not one of them.

On the contrary, boxer cool is *hot*—a culturally derived repertoire of looks, stances and gestures acquired over time, crucial to navigating lived structural and physical violence, and decisive for managing the seething frustration and reifying indignation resulting from such violence. In boxer cool, elements, lessons, and know-how from the world of 'the hood' are recalibrated and effectively redeployed in the context of training and competing in the sport. Boxer cool is thus derivative of a milieu where individuals must learn to self-manage the complex emotional states and potential conflicts continually emergent in the

28 *Boxing and culture*

physical and structural violence endemic to their daily life. Boxer cool, in other words, finds its immediate origins not primarily in the gym or ring but in the necessary cultivation of sophisticated orientations, coping mechanisms, and practices of self-management in persistently dangerous and harmful contexts.

For cool is simultaneously noun, adjective, and verb in 'the hood'. It is a way-of-being and being-known—a bearing of self-mastery that demands to be recognized in urban locations of physical and structural disrespect and deprivation. In this regard, we should emphasize that cool is far more than an aesthetic; fundamentally, it is a street-level stance or cultural pose.[2] Inasmuch as it contains complexly embedded and embodied displays of self-possession and stored aggression, cool at once threatens, veils, and diffuses. Moreover, it plays an important role in staving off or resolving violent conflicts in controlled ways, as we shall see directly. Put differently, in contexts where struggles for status and respect are especially acute, cool is a currency—a kind of cultural capital in the form of a look or posture or comportment—the value of which resides in its power to ward off potential threats, manage fear, command respect, and regulate the temperature, as it were, of street-level confrontations and disputes. In fact, having the right look or adopting the appropriate orientations at the right times and in the right ways—being cool and getting cool with others—is crucial to getting on in a world of physical and structural violence.

Hence, properly understood, boxer cool is part of a broader urban cultural code—what Elijah Anderson (1999) has called the 'code of the street'. Most generally, in his ethnographic study of Philadelphia, Anderson argues that this 'street code' consists of the unwritten rules (norms) of comportment that loosely govern struggles for respect and status in 'the ghetto'. Or, as he puts the matter: 'At the heart of the code is the issue of respect—loosely defined as being treated "right" or being granted one's "props" (or proper due) or the deference one deserves' (Anderson 1999, 33). Put briefly: Anderson's research demonstrates how the code of the street constrains (and enables) the many ways in which respect is negotiated and (re)produced among 'ghetto' residents.

In doing so, his work provides a rich ethnographic resource for fleshing out a conception of boxer cool and, indeed, the affinities between urban cultural practices and the sport of boxing proper. To be sure, Anderson draws no connection between the code of the street and anything akin to 'boxer cool'—or the sport of boxing, for that matter—but his account of the 'social meaning of fighting'

(Anderson 1999, 69) is immediately relevant for any study of the intersection of urban culture and the sport of boxing.

Indeed, in the following passage, devoted to the description of a confrontation between Tyree and Malik (two young residents of South Philadelphia), cool (understood as part of a street code) and boxing begin to congeal in the fistic but controlled resolution of a slight Tyree perceives as the two of them flirt with some local young women:

'Say, man. ... You always dissin' me. I'm tired of yo' shit, man', says Tyree.

'Aw, man. I didn't do nothin', responds Malik.

'Yes you did....I'm tired of yo' shit. Put up yo' hands, man. Put up you' hands', challenges Tyree.

'Aw, man, I don't wanta fight you, man', responds Malik.

'Naw, man. I ain't bullshittin'. Put up yo' hands', presses Tyree. The two men walk behind the building where they are standing and begin to square off. Almost on cue, the two friends put up their hands in the fighting position ... Tyree and Malik have agreed to a contest that is somewhere between a fair fight and a real fight. ... Such fights are characterized by elaborate rules, including 'no hitting in the face', 'you got to use just your hands', and 'no double-teaming' ... Malik and Tyree dance and spar, huffing and puffing, dodging and feinting. To the onlooker, it appears to be a game, for real blows seem hardly to be exchanged. But suddenly Malik lands a blow to Tyree's shoulder and another to his stomach...dropping his guard, Tyree acknowledges this, but then quickly resumes his fighting stance ... they go at it again, punching, dancing, dodging. Tyree lands a good punch to Malik's stomach and then, with a right cross, catches him on the chest, but Malik counters with a kidney punch and a knee to the crotch. Tyree checks his opponent with, 'Watch that shit, man' ... Tyree, hands up, accidentally lands an open hand to Malik's face with the sound of a slap. Tyree knows...that he has violated the rules of the fair fight, and just as quickly he says, 'Aw, 'cuse me, man' ... Malik responds, 'Watch yourself, man. Watch yourself'.

They continue their dancing and sparring for about 20 minutes and then stop. They have fought and, for the moment, settled their differences. But, actually, something much more profound has occurred as well...Through this little fight...they have tested each other's mettle, discerned important limits, and gained an abiding sense of what each one will 'take' from the other. With this in mind they adjust their behavior in each other's presence, giving the other his 'props', or respect...*Essentially, this is what it means to 'get cool' with someone*...(Anderson 1999, 89–91, emphasis added)

There are, to be sure, many things to note in the above ethnographic excerpt. But three aspects are of particular interest in the present context. The first thing to stress is that the dispute centers not on money or drugs or clothes but rather on *disrespect*. Tyree perceives that he has been 'dissed' by Malik in a way that has negative implications for his store of symbolic capital (status) and personal estimation (recognition). Second although a physical confrontation is immanent and seemingly unavoidable, the two do not resort to violence willy-nilly. Instead, in a seemingly effortless display of self-mastery (almost 'on cue', as Anderson says), the two reflexively calibrate and channel the heat of their conflict through an elaborately articulated kind of proto-sparring session. Third, and finally, while we would not go so far as to call this an engagement in the *sport* of boxing—or even boxing *training*—the live combat is in fact clearly informed by constitutive (if emergent) rules and flexible constraints that enable and limit the level and kind of violence that may be used here.

Tyree and Malik do not find themselves in a 'play' boxing match. Their 'fight' is both real and symbolic—it is a culturally mitigated form of violence coded in ways that 'to the onlooker' make it appear to be 'a game', as Anderson notes. But this is not chess or checkers; nor is it mere dramatic artifice. The stakes are high and the failure to restore an equilibrium of status and respect between Tyree and Malik could prove fatal. To avoid such a fate, each must refrain from 'going off' (losing self-control) and instead maintain the self-mastery of something akin to pugilistic nonchalance—as Tyree tellingly does in boxer-like style when he drops his guard to acknowledge (and thereby dismiss) the effects of a cleanly landed combination. Such high stakes nonchalance must be preserved even (especially) when, in the absence of a referee, the two youths mutually remind and correct one another about the inadmissibility of 'rule violations', such as when Malik lands a low blow or Tyree face-slaps Malik.

Now, in the broadest of terms, for our purposes here the significance of all this is twofold. At the cultural level, the fight between Tyree and Malik makes explicit how struggles for status and respect in the urban milieu are often informed by an epistemology of cool that feeds, albeit in modified form, into the sport of boxing. Tyree and Malik are not boxers, to be sure, but in their confrontation with one another we see key features and functions of boxer cool come into sharp focus. At the structural level, the fight itself can and should in many ways be read as a cultural precursor to some of what goes on in an actual boxing gym, particularly during sparring sessions.[3] Though their fight is oriented explicitly toward cultural ends (respect and status) rather than athletic ones (excellence and victory), structurally speaking the contest between Tyree and Malik nevertheless has profound parallels with the kind of pugilistic nonchalance one sees in contemporary combat sports. Indeed, the proximity between the fistic way in which they resolve their dispute and 'get cool' with one another and elements of the sport of boxing is unmistakable.

The sketch of pugilistic nonchalance developed here is of course not designed to characterize all boxers—or, indeed, anything like the necessary cultural conditions to becoming a boxer. There are, of course, many cultural pathways into the sport, none of which is essential. Yet boxer cool is a form of urban culture athletically sublimated in ways one does not see in many other sports. The concept of boxer cool aims to capture the complex interplay of culture and sport specifically in urban contexts where physical and structural violence pervade daily life. Elaborating a conception of boxer cool provides the makings of a culturally informed (but not reductive) explanation for how and why some individuals, through culturally informed reflexive practices of self-mastery, are oriented to and able to navigate the threats of danger and harm peculiar to pugilism.

Moreover, when considered alongside the notion of pugilistic selfhood outlined previously, the conception of boxer cool presented here also helps to explain the gap between (often subpar) athleticism and persistence in the sport of professional boxing. For individuals who persist in the gym and manage to become pro boxers are, as I saw firsthand at Authentic Boxing, often not the best athletes. Instead, those that make it are highly reflexive *street code adapters*. They successfully reconfigure and rehabituate cool—thus internalizing Coach Edgar's reproach that the gym 'ain't no ghetto'—not by rejecting the lessons of 'the hood' but by modifying and redeploying their knowledge of the code of the street within the confines of a most perilous athletic endeavor.

Notes

1 In other words, in the case of boxing, especially, there is a profound cultural dimension to what Russell (2005) has aptly characterized as the value of 'self-affirmation' peculiar to dangerous sport.

2 For an explicit discussion of cool and masculine culture in African–American contexts, see especially Majors and Billson (1992) and Hooks (2004). And for a related discussion in the context of British boxing, see especially Woodward (2004, 2007). In the present context, we must emphasize that while boxer cool may typically be gendered 'masculine', it is not necessarily or in any determinative way thusly gendered. Female residents of difficult urban contexts, not unlike and perhaps even more so than their male counterparts, must develop a repertoire of practical orientations vis-à-vis violence (both physical and structural) and do indeed redeploy those orientations in the sport of boxing, as I saw Franchesca and other female boxers at Authentic do repeatedly.

3 The subject of sparring is one to which we shall return in some detail in the second part of this study.

References

Anderson, Elijah. 1999. *Code of the Street: Decency, Violence, and the Moral Life of the Inner City*. New York: Norton.

Hooks, Bell. 2004. *We Real Cool: Black Men and Masculinity*. New York: Routledge.

Howe, Leslie A. 2004. 'Gamesmanship.' *Journal of the Philosophy of Sport* 31 (2): 212–225.

Leota, Josh and Michael-John Turp. 2020. 'Gamesmanship as Strategic Excellence.' *Journal of the Philosophy of Sport* 47 (2): 232–247.

Majors, Richard and Janet Mancini Billson. 1992. *Cool Pose: The Dilemmas of Black Manhood in America*. New York: Lexington.

Russell, John. 2005. 'The Value of Dangerous Sport.' *Journal of the Philosophy of Sport* 32 (1): 1–19.

Wiley, Ralph. 1989. *Serenity: A Boxing Memoir*. Lincoln, NE: University of Nebraska Press.

Woodward, Kath. 2004. 'Rumbles in the Jungle: Boxing, Racialization, and the Performance of Masculinity.' *Leisure Studies* 23 (1): 5–17.

Woodward, Kath. 2007. *Boxing, Masculinity and Identity: The 'I' of the Tiger*. New York: Routledge.

4 Boxing and social capital?

In analyses of pugilistic selfhood, structural and physical violence, and the conception of 'boxer cool', the previous chapters have sought to examine the urban cultural embeddedness of the sport of boxing. Taken together, these aspects of the cultural dimensions of pugilism were meant to suggest the profound extent to which the sport of boxing intersects with and, indeed, athletically sublimates, culturally informed struggles and practices in the urban milieu. In this chapter, I want to consider a related but somewhat different question, namely, the social nature and functions of what goes on in an urban boxing gym. More specifically, I want to inquire about the nature of the social effects of participation in the sport of boxing. Put generally, the issue to be addressed in what follows is whether, along with the cultural capital produced by and (re)deployed in becoming a boxer, there aren't unique forms of socialization emergent in a boxing club.

As a point of reference to address the question about boxing and the social, it is instructive to turn to the work of Robert Putnam, whose social capital theorizing has been widely influential in a variety of disciplines and policy-making in the United States and elsewhere.[1] As is well known, for Putnam, social capital—understood broadly as networks, norms, ties, and trust that 'bond' and 'bridge' individuals together in various ways—can be produced in and through participation in sport, particularly team sport, and is crucial to 'making democracy work'. The core idea seems to be that there is political (democratic) value (capital) causally generated by team sport engagement, inasmuch as team sport, according to Putnam, 'bridges' together a diversity of individuals to form communities beyond individual identities. In fact, in his view, it is in the team sport of bowling (among other communal forms, such as singing in a choir) that we humans are required to '*transcend* our social and political and professional identities and connect with people *unlike ourselves* ... Singing

DOI: 10.4324/9781003196693-4

together (like bowling together) does not require shared ideology or shared social or ethnic provenance' (Putnam 2000, 411, emphasis added).

In this chapter, I want to focus on bowling and boxing to scrutinize such an assertion about the transcendent 'bridging' power of participation in sport.[2] Historically speaking, bowling alleys and bowling leagues do not exist in a socioeconomic vacuum; like boxing clubs, they are embedded in and informed by broader societal structures and forces, as I hope to show. Moreover, while it is evident that team sports foster collective actions of various kinds, and may even generate a vague sense of belonging, competitive sport teamwork is nevertheless characteristically stratified by skill, position, game day requirements, and so on.[3] To paraphrase Michael Jordan, while there may be 'No "I" in "team", there is an 'I/i' in "win"'. Contra Putnam, then, on both historical and normative grounds appeals to the transcendent ('democratic') effects of team sport participation are difficult to defend. Consequently, the argument to be pursued here is that in connecting sport and the social, we must guard against the kind of causal claims and moral inflationism found in Putnam's thinking about bowling.

That is not to say that sports such as bowling or boxing have no desirable social effects. Rather, it is simply to suggest that those effects do not necessarily transcend sport participation in ways that contribute to democracy or identity-transcending communities. The relationship between sport and the social is far more nuanced than Putnam's social capital theorizing and Putnamian-inspired policy-making allow. This is the case not only in an individual combat sport like boxing but, even, in fact, in the team sport of bowling, which Putnam takes as a paradigmatic example of the transcendent potential of social capital production in sport.

The link between sport and social capital is often made using the associated term of 'community'.[4] Indeed, Putnam himself repeatedly conflates social capital with community—what he calls 'the conceptual cousin' (Putnam 2000, 21) of social capital. This is not surprising, as the concept of community and its revival is one of the main subtexts of Putnam's work, in which calls for 'reviving' and 'restoring' 'the American community' have played a prominent role for decades. Putnam's affinity for the democratic power of community stems from his reading of Alexander de Tocqueville and Tocqueville's account of the shared 'can-do' habits and voluntary 'techniques of association' (Tocqueville, 1969, 522) peculiar to the *citoyen* of 19th-century American communities. In fact, Putnam weaves Tocqueville into his account of social capital and democracy to suggest that the 'voluntary associations ... we have been calling "social capital" contribute to democracy in two different ways: they have "external" effects on the larger polity, and they have "internal" effects on the participants themselves' (Putnam 2000, 338).

Though presented as an empirical study of declining participation rates in sport and other associational forms of civil society, repeated attempts, however strained, to demonstrate the 'external' normative efficacy of social capital production punctuate Putnam's work. Perhaps one of the most telling examples of this appears early on in *Bowling Alone*, when, in an effort to illustrate the effects of 'bridging social capital' in sport, Putnam anecdotally recounts the story of two men—one Black, the other White—who formerly bowled together on a team (Putnam 2000, 28). According to Putnam, John Lambert (an older African-American) and Andy Boschma (a younger White-American) bowled together in a league at the Ypsi-Arbor Lanes in Michigan. Boschma, as Putnam recounts the story, 'learned casually of Lambert's need [for a kidney] and ... unexpectedly approached him to offer to donate one of his own kidneys' (Putnam 2000, 28). Putnam links this impromptu life-saving kidney donation directly and causally to the power of the 'bridging social capital' generated by team bowling; indeed, he claims that the mere fact 'that they bowled together made all the difference' (Putnam 2000, 28).

Kind though Mr. Boschma's idiosyncratic act may have been, it is difficult to see how interracial (and intergenerational) kidney donations have much to do with the putatively transcendent power of participation in the sport of bowling.[5] To be sure, bowling was indeed a popular sport among many kinds of people in America. By the mid-1960s, it is estimated that there were more than 12,000 bowling centers in the United States. At that time nearly all individual bowlers competed on teams in established local leagues whose seasons involved weekly competitions over the course of at least 30 weeks of every year.

Yet it is an exercise in overstatement to say that participation in team bowling, however popular during that sport's heyday, produced social capital or durable communal forms that consistently 'bridged' or 'transcended' the structural forces of ethnicity and class in the United States. In fact, Putnam's tale of 'vanishing social capital'—and the concomitant decline of community and democracy—in the demise of team bowling in the United States is historically reductive. Bowling for African-Americans was segregated under Jim Crow laws in the United States, and remained that way in the de facto segregation that followed. The sport reflected and augmented—and continues to reflect and augment—a kind of de facto apartheid in many sectors of

America life. Black Americans bowled in 'basements', while White Americans bowled in proper bowling alleys.[6] Excluded from joining and competing in the American Bowling Congress until 1951, Black Americans formed their own bowling league in 1939. Initially know as National Negro Bowling Association, the organization subsequently changed its name to The National Bowling Association (TNBA). Even today, with more than 30,000 members and 115 affiliates in the United States and Bermuda, the TNBA remains a profoundly ethnoracially homogenous sport association, with African-Americans comprising over 80% of its membership.[7] Thus bowling among African-Americans may generate 'Black social capital', to borrow Orr's (1999) phrase, but it does not foster—and, historically, clearly has not fostered—anything like the transcendent 'bridging social capital' attributed to it by Putnam.

Moreover, today bowling (among Blacks and Whites) is also increasingly stratified by income in the United States. In fact, with the costs associated with multi-million dollar bowling and entertainment centers, the sport has become primarily an upper-middle-class form of individual recreation. Recreational and 'party' bowling are a ten-billion-dollar industry in the United States, one oriented well beyond the reach of most working class people. Indeed, data indicate that 42% of bowlers in the United States come from household incomes of $75,000 or higher, while those with earnings of $100,000 or higher account for slightly more than 25% of all bowlers.[8]

Thus, in America the sport of bowling decidedly did not function as a broad-based 'bridge' that connected ethnoracially or socioeconomically diverse groups. On the contrary, by and large African–Americans (like their White counterparts) continued—and to this day still continue—to bowl and compete with 'others' *like themselves*. The argument would seem to hold economically as well: upper middle-income earners bowl, 'party', and compete with other upper middle-income earners. The point is not that sport participation lacks social effects. But those effects cannot be normatively overloaded or assumed to be community diversifying or democratizing in any necessary way. Putnam is correct to suggest that participation in a sport like bowling does not *require* shared social or ethnoracial provenance. But neither does bowling necessarily serve to diversify such provenances in transcendent or externalizing ways consistent with or causally related to diverse community building or democracy.

Can the same be said of boxing? As a violent individual combat sport with a very different ethnoracial history, boxing is not akin to team bowling.[9] With its low (nearly non-existent) economic barriers to entry and participation, the relatively modest cost of maintaining a no frills working boxing gym, and minimal amounts of money at stake in most local and regional competitions, access to and participation in boxing diverges in important respects from a sport like bowling. And unlike bowling, the sport of boxing, at least in American urban contexts, *does* in fact consistently bring together an ethnoracially diverse group of women and men to train and compete with one another.

Yet it does so in complex and even contradictory ways that may connect but do not 'transcend' an ethnoracially diverse pool of athletes. Boxers do not generally think of themselves as a colorblind community. On the contrary, as victims of structural violence boxers know and 'see color', as the saying goes, *in themselves and their opponents*. This kind of acute ethnoracial awareness—both implicit and explicit—is pervasive in boxing and can become apparent in the gym and/or in the lead up to fights. In recent memory perhaps the most well-known case of this was in the 2008 'Battle of the Planet' between Bernard Hopkins and Joe Calzaghe. Leading up to that fight, which was fought for Hopkins' light heavyweight title, Hopkins and Calzaghe engaged in a public shouting match, with Hopkins scorning Calzaghe not merely for his skills but also for who he was: 'You're not even in my league! I would never let a White boy beat me. I would never lose to a White boy. I couldn't go back to the projects if I let a White boy beat me'.[10]

Such a comment must not be construed merely as an attempt to generate interest in an upcoming match—or even 'trash talk' in a more general sense. For it is no accident that Hopkins called Calzaghe a '*White boy*' and not, say, a Welsh man. It is similarly no accident that Hopkins linked his success in the fight to his status and respect in '*the projects*' ('ghetto' or 'hood'), rather than, say, his win-loss record as a pro boxer or his prospect for future big-money fights. Boxers are highly ethnoracially conscious, and often draw on, hybridize, and/or hyper-exaggerate ethnoracial identities—as Aaron at Authentic Boxing did by nicknaming himself 'The Blaxican', for example.[11] Indeed, in boxing such ethnoracialization informs how individual boxers chose their nicknames, ring walk costuming and music, and even their style of fighting. It also extends to how they conceive of other boxers. At the level of identity, that is to say, in boxing individuals do not to join or compete in an identity-transcending community but instead fashion a pugilistic selfhood from *within* a particular cultural milieu where ethnoracial identities are characteristically made explicit; recall the telling line that captioned the locker room poster of Dennis and Muhammad Ali found at Authentic: 'he was just another skinny *Black* kid once, too'.

Consequently, rather than attempt to connect boxing to a Putnamian notion of 'bridging social capital', it is more productive to think of boxing and combat athletics in general as fostering potential sites of embodied and embedded 'sociation'.[12] In contrast to the 'transcendent' conception of bridging social capital, sociation more precisely describes the social function of boxing.[13] Sociation is repeated human interaction and cooperation in a distilled form. Boxing clubs are both athletic places to train (gymnasia) and complex *sites of sociation* (loci of repeated cooperative action).

Now, generally speaking, sites of sociation in sport can function horizontally and/or vertically. Sporting sites of horizontal sociation are largely accessible and appropriable by individuals from within a specific socioeconomic, cultural, and/or ethnoracial stratum. In this homogeneous form of sociation in sport, which is most common, individuals engage with 'others' more or less *like* themselves. Bowling in America is a prime example, as we have seen. Sites of vertical sociation, by contrast, are largely accessible and appropriable by individuals from up and down existing socioeconomic, cultural, and/or ethnoracial strata. In this heterogeneous form of sociation, which is fairly uncommon, individuals engage with 'Others' more or less *unlike* themselves.

In the sport of boxing, one often sees both horizontal and vertical features of sociation simultaneously. In fact, in my experience, in ethnoracial terms Authentic Boxing proved to be a fairly durable site of vertical sociation—with boxers divided loosely among three different ethnoracial groups. Yet economically, the gym was a site of horizontal sociation—with most boxers employed in low-level and semi-skilled jobs. This kind of cross-cutting sociation is characteristic in the sport of boxing (and combat sport more widely), which often draws individuals (regardless of ethnoracial identity) accustomed to physical labor, embodied professional crafts, fear and violence and/or fluent in 'street codes' of various kinds.

Yet we should be modest about the kinds of normative effects we ascribe to sociation—in both its commonplace horizontal and the more exceptional vertical forms. For the effects of sociation are not necessarily or even primarily external. Becoming a boxer (or bowler, for that matter) doesn't necessarily make one a better citizen; but neither are the effects of participation in boxing morally trivial. For boxing clubs are sites that demand and cultivate constrained individuality (self-mastery) and cooperatively shared commitments to mutual betterment.[14] Certain desirable externalities may result from such sociation, to be sure. Some boxers, like many other athletes, may transfer their newly fashioned identities and cooperative social habits acquired in sport participation to wider societal contexts. I take this possibility to be one of the primary driving factors for community development through youth sport, for example.[15] But there is no—and there need not be any—*necessary connection* between sociation in sport and this kind of broader external effect on community, social capital production, or 'making democracy work'.

In sum, the short answer to the question about boxing and social capital is that we should be skeptical about too strongly connecting participation in boxing to transcendent 'bridging' social effects that realize community or democracy. As the loci for honing skilled violence, athletically sublimating struggles for recognition and respect, and cultivating boxer cool, boxing clubs can hardly be expected to serve as academies of democracy. Instead, as I have tried to suggest in this chapter via a critical engagement with Putnam's thinking about bowling and social capital, the question of the social function of combat sport like boxing is better answered using the concept of sociation. Boxing gyms and, I would maintain, combat sport clubs in general, are unique venues for types of embodied and embedded sociation—horizontal and vertical—that foster self-mastery and a cooperative ethos aimed at mutual betterment. Hence, the distinct capacity to function as a site of horizontal *and* vertical sociation does not lend boxing anything like a democratic function, but it does suggest a cross-cutting social effect of pugilism not found in bowling or, indeed, participation in many other sports.

Notes

1 Of course Putnam's work is not the only one of relevance in a discussion of sport and social capital. The work of Pierre Bourdieu, especially, is also noteworthy in this regard. Elsewhere I have developed a more thoroughgoing study of social capital (Lewandowski 2006) that critically engages the work of Putnam, Bourdieu, and Coleman to identify three strands in social capital thinking. In the interest of space and focus on sport participation and community in the US context I limit my discussion here to core themes in Putnam.
2 In a related vein I have questioned Putnam's 'bridging' and 'bonding' concepts of social capital and their link to democracy by arguing that it is not social capital the produces democracy but rather social capital (re)production and circulation that is in need of democratization (Lewandowski and Streich 2007).
3 But for a rich account of teamwork in sport developed outside the framework of social capital, see especially Gaffney (2014).

4 See especially Nicholson and Hoye (2008), in particular the chapters collected in sections II and III.
5 Indeed, as Putnam relates the anecdote it does not even seem that these two gentlemen were friends, as Boschma 'learned casually' and not directly from Lambert about latter's need for a kidney.
6 For a rich historical account of 'basement bowling', see especially Cherland (2016).
7 Membership data taken from TNBA website: www.tnbainc.org.
8 White Hutchison Leisure and Learning Group (2011, 2015).
9 In the US context, boxing was not so much an ethnoracially exclusionary sport but rather an arena for the physical and symbolic struggles between and among different groups for ethnoracial superiority, as evidenced in, for example, Ward (2004).
10 'Projects' is a slang term for the high-density low-income and federally subsidized public housing complexes or 'estates' prominent in many US ghettos.
11 One sees this in other combat sports as well. Mixed Martial Arts features, for example, Derrick Lewis, a professional African-American fighter nicknamed, 'The Black Beast'.
12 I borrow this conception of *Geselligkeit* ('sociation' or 'sociability'), albeit loosely, from Simmel (1949), and have elsewhere developed a more extensive account of sociability and its harnessing or 'capitalization' (Lewandowski 2006) in human interactions of various kinds. Wacquant (2004) also alludes to how boxing gyms function as sites of sociability, but he does not develop this point in the context of a critique of social capital and sport.
13 But for a more Bourdieuean account of boxing and social capital, see Fulton (2011), whose ethnography focuses on social (and bodily) capital (re)production in a British boxing gym.
14 This claim is one we shall return to in chapter 8.
15 Though in light of its high risk for concussive head injuries, it must be acknowledged that boxing is hardly a preferred choice for a community development approach to youth sport participation.

References

Cherland, Summer. 2016. 'Basement Bowlers: The National Negro Bowling Association and Its Legacy of Black Leadership.' In *Separate Games: African-American Sport Behind the Walls of Segregation*, edited by David K. Wiggins and Ryan A. Swanson, 203–218. Fayetteville, AK: University of Arkansas Press.
Fulton, John. 2011. '"What's Your Worth?": The Development of Capital in British Boxing.' *European Journal for Sport and Society* 8 (3): 193–218.
Gaffney, Paul. 2014. 'The Nature and Meaning of Teamwork.' *Journal of the Philosophy of Sport* 42 (1): 1–22.
Lewandowski, Joseph. 2006. 'Capitalizing Sociability: Rethinking the Theory of Social Capital.' In *Assessing Social Capital: Concepts, Policy, and*

Practice, edited by Rosalind Edwards, Jane Franklin, and Janet Holland, 14–28. New Castle: Cambridge Scholars Publishing.

Lewandowski, Joseph and Gregory Streich. 2007. 'Democratizing Social Capital: In Pursuit of Liberal Egalitarianism.' *Journal of Social Philosophy* 38 (3): 588–604.

Nicholson, Matthew and Russell Hoye, eds. 2008. *Sport and Social Capital.* Oxford: Elsevier.

Orr, Marion. 1999. *Black Social Capital: The Politics of School Reform in Baltimore, 1986-1998.* Lawrence, KS: University of Kansas Press.

Putnam, Robert. 2000. *Bowling Alone: The Collapse and Revival of American Community.* New York: Simon and Schuster.

Simmel, Georg. 1949. 'The Sociology of Sociability.' *American Journal of Sociology* 55 (2): 254–268.

Tocqueville, Alexis. 1969. *Democracy in America*, trans. G. Lawrence. New York: Harper.

Wacquant, L. (2004) *Body and Soul: Notebooks of an Apprentice Boxer.* Oxford: Oxford University Press.

Ward, Geoffrey C. 2004. *Unforgiveable Blackness: The Rise and Fall of Jack Johnson.* New York: Knopf.

White Hutchison Leisure and Learning Group. 2011. Accessed 15 June 2021. https://www.whitehutchinson.com/news/lenews/2011/august/article107-bowling-trend.shtml

White Hutchison Leisure and Learning Group. 2015. Accessed 15 June 2021. https://www.whitehutchinson.com/leisure/articles/downloads/bowling-paradox-of-two-worlds.pdf

5 The marginality of urban boxing clubs

With its founding in 1998, the continued survival of Authentic Boxing club is nothing short of extraordinary. For urban boxing gyms have a precarious existence—and for a variety of reasons. Along with the rise in 'hobby' or 'white collar' boxing competitions, the sport itself has been significantly commodified by a culture industry built around fitness and health.[1] Indeed, while working boxing gyms are a vanishing breed in most American cities, one need not look far to find 'fitness boxing' gyms, which tend to be located in better neighborhoods, charge high fees, and serve a privileged clientele very much unlike the men and women who train at Authentic and other local urban clubs throughout the United States. It is estimated that over five million people in the United States participate in some form of fitness boxing.[2] By contrast, there are approximately 18,000 licensed professional boxers worldwide, about 3,200 of whom reside in the United States.[3] In the past several years in the Kansas City area, Title Boxing (a local boxing gear maker) has franchised its name and opened Title Boxing Club fitness centers in six locations in the metropolitan region, and over 170 clubs nationwide. More recently, Kansas City has also seen competing national boxing fitness chains, such as 9RoundFitness and Mayweather Boxing + Fitness, move into the area.

Yet such gyms are not *boxing clubs* in any sporting sense of the term. Instead, they are, like most health and fitness clubs in the United States, designed explicitly as revenue-generating businesses that cater to an ethnoracially homogenous (White) leisured class. The commodity they sell is a particular kind of 'experience'—a 'no touch fitness experience', as Title Boxing Club calls it—designed to mimic the non-contact elements of boxers' actual training regimes with bag drills, high-intensity interval cardio, and individualized personal training sessions. In what is surely a national trend, these fitness boxing clubs already outnumber actual boxing gyms in Kansas City; in fact, as

DOI: 10.4324/9781003196693-5

working boxing gyms dedicated to the *sport* of boxing fail they are increasingly replaced by Title Boxing Club and other health club franchises dedicated explicitly to boxing fitness training. As this process accelerates, actual boxing gyms become ever more marginal. Indeed, in the fitnessization of boxing, the sport is distorted into a kind of privileged leisure activity.

At the same time, at the competitive level over the last decade or so, the sport of boxing has been extensively absorbed into the hugely successful combat sport of MMA. Indeed, while Authentic Boxing is a boxing-only club, it is largely the exception in the competitive fight scene today. In fact, several working boxing gyms in the Kansas City area are now MMA clubs, where athletes train in boxing, Muay Thai, and Jiu-Jitsu, among other martial arts forms.[4] This is a national trend, as individuals (especially women) who once would have pursued competitive boxing now look to MMA—or to compete in both MMA and boxing—as professional combat sport athletes. In this way, the meteoric rise of MMA has hybridized and largely subsumed the sport of boxing.

The twin pressures of the culture industry (fitnessization) and MMA (hybridization) are, to be sure, not the only forces that threaten the continued existence of working boxing clubs in the American urban milieu. The precarity of most American boxing gyms predates such pressures, and stems unmistakably from their historical and ethnoracial embeddness in 'the hood'. Most urban boxing clubs, that is to say, are squeezed by the contemporary market forces of the fitness industry and MMA on one side, and, on the other side, by their place in the kind of structural violence of ghettoization and neoliberalization examined previously.

In this chapter, I want to close the discussion of boxing and culture by returning to those earlier themes and connecting them to the plight of a famous boxing gym, Joe Frazier's Gym, located in North Philadelphia. For the contemporary fate of Frazier's gym stands as a kind of allegory for much of the sport of boxing today—a marginalized sport situated in a marginalized (and failing) life-world. It also serves as a point of contrast for the fragile but continued existence of a gym like Authentic Boxing.

The story of North Philly is a not an unfamiliar one in urban America. In the early part of the 20th century, industrialization in the city triggered rapid population growth. This in turn altered the urban landscape of the city, as the spacious gridiron design of North Philly came to be subdivided into smaller parcels on which brick row houses were constructed to accommodate the growing housing needs of working-class families. Growth and development in the area was fueled by an expanding industrial and manufacturing base, immigration of labor from Europe, and, especially, heavy internal migration of African-American families from the rural south to the industrializing north. Thus by the mid-1900s, an industrial-institutional ghetto had firmly rooted itself in North Philadelphia.

It was in the flow of this familiar American urban narrative that, several decades later, a century-old, 30,000 square feet former lumber warehouse on 2917 North Broad Street caught the eye of Joe Frazier and his management company, Cloverlay. In the late 1960s, Frazier, who was born in Beaufort, South Carolina, had been looking for a good place to train. The space was converted and initially opened as the 'Cloverlay Gym' in 1968 but was renamed 'Joe Frazier's Gym' thereafter; indeed, in the limestone cornice that separates the stucco and limestone base of the building from the brick upper floors the engraving, 'Joe Frazier's Gym', can still be seen clearly.

Frazier trained in this location for the duration of his pugilistic career. It was here that he prepared himself for what were to be career-defining fights with Ali and Foreman, among others. During those training camps, Frazier was also known to live above the gym on the 3rd floor of the warehouse. After his retirement in 1976, Frazier modified the 3rd floor space above the gym. Originally an open floor plan, the space was loosely divided, using floor-to-ceiling curtains, into residential spaces, including a makeshift kitchen, a gypsum board enclosed bathroom, and carpeting throughout. Cramped and grubby though it was, for the remainder of his life Frazier made the space his permanent home as he dedicated himself to the gym and his adopted North Philly 'hood'.[5]

And a 'hood' it had indeed become. For Frazier's arrival and opening of a boxing gym in North Philly in the late 1960s did not happen in an unremarkable period in the history of that 'ghetto' and so many others like it in the United States. On the contrary, already at that time Philadelphia's industrial and manufacturing economy began to fail; North Philly's industrial-institutional ghetto was slowly becoming a jobless post-industrial ghetto. In fact, by the 1980s, the area around Frazier's Gym, referred to as 'the Badlands' by local residents, was in physical decay and steep socio-economic decline as it succomed to the oppressive forces of the kind of structural violence discussed earlier.

The available US Census data make this point explicit in a particularly dire set of statistics. The gym's urban milieu ('the Badlands') is home to measurable but almost unspeakable levels of structural violence. 36,268 people live in 'the Badlands', 94% of whom are African-American and 52% of whom are unemployed. The district's median household income is $18,777USD for a family of four; the state-wide household median for a family of four is $40,106USD. Average house values currently hover around $25,000USD, and the housing unit vacancy rate approaches 25%. Only 36% of 'Badlands' dwellers have earned high school diplomas.

By any measure, the local school, George Clymer Elementary, is in a perpetual state of fiscal and academic crisis. In Pennsylvania state administered standardized testing, only 28% of Clymer Elementary School's 8th grade students perform at grade level in math, while an even lower percentage (14%) manage to achieve satisfactorily in science. And more than half (58%) of all 8th grade students at the school are unable to read and write at grade level.

In 2008 Joe Frazier's Gym was closed. It was subsequently sold to British boxer Marianne Martson, who had relocated from London to Philadelphia to train under Frazier and his son, Marvis. In 2011, Joe Frazier's Gym was listed for sale with an asking price of $999,000USD—a price it was not to realize. Thanks in part to the interests of a local professor of architecture, Dennis Playdon, and some of his graduate students at nearby Temple University, the fate of the property gained national media attention with a campaign to 'save' Frazier's gym. In 2012 the building was added to the register of America's 11 Most Endangered Historical Places by the National Trust for Historic Preservation. In 2013, the site was finally placed on the National Register of Historic Places. Such a designation protects the gym from adverse alterations or demolition in perpetuity. In other words, Joe Frazier's Gym is now a kind of state-protected monument located in a part of Philadelphia that few non-residents are likely ever to visit. The irony cannot be overstated: Joe Frazier's Gym has become a building protected by a national agency devoted to historical preservation in a 'hood' that itself almost certainly will *not* be saved by the state.

There are, to be sure, personal reasons that partially explain why Frazier's Gym failed so dramatically. Frazier, who lost the building as compensation for unpaid taxes, was, like most boxers, not much of a businessman, and surrounded himself with less than honest personal and financial advisers. But in light of the overarching position outlined in the previous chapters, it would be a mistake to attribute the demise of this historic boxing gym to the personal failings of one man. Indeed, it has been one of the core arguments of this book that an adequate understanding of the sport of boxing depends in no small way on a grasp of the urban milieu in which it is embedded. Joe Frazier's Gym did not fail simply because of Joe Frazier's weak business acumen; indeed, if that were the case then one might have expected to see his gym leased by investors looking to transform it into a cleverly branded fitness boxing club, for example. Nor does it appear to be a likely site for a future working boxing gym. In fact, Joe Hand, the charter shareholder of Cloverlay (Frazier's original management company), recently opened 'Joe Hand Boxing Gym' in Feasterville, Pennsylvania, *some 15 miles (and 45 minutes) drive north of Frazier's former gym in 'the Badlands'*.

The core point to be made, by way of concluding this section, is that urban boxing gyms in the United States characteristically fail when the life-world around them collapses. This is why a boxing club like Joe Frazier's Gym—one with a distinct pedigree located in a city known for boxing—failed, while a modest gym like Authentic Boxing continues to hang on, however precariously and by financially obscure means. Urban boxing clubs are marginalized homes to a marginalized sport in the United States. In the case of the demise of Joe Frazier's Gym, what sets 'the Badlands' apart is the sheer advancement of its marginality as a 'hood'. By contrast, in the case of Authentic Boxing, while the boxers who train there inhabit locations not unlike 'the Badlands', the gym itself is located in a largely non-residential urban warehouse district that has not similarly collapsed. Thus for the moment, at least, the relentless ruination of 'the Badlands' in Philadelphia stands in relative contrast to the stubborn persistence of the West Bottoms in Kansas City. Depending on a variety of factors Athentic Boxing may indeed succumb to a similar fate—or, what appears more likely, be priced out of its milieu through gentrification, and perhaps even remade as a fitness boxing gym for future local loft dwellers. In any case, the inescapable fact remains that boxing is perhaps the most marginal of professional combat sports. Indeed, in the United States, a boxing gym's fate is ineluctably entwined with larger forces—such as the fitness culture industry, the MMA market, gentrification pressures, and structural violence—at work in the city in which it is situated.

Notes

1 For a glimpse of the popularity of the contemporary scene in white collar boxing in the United States, see especially Gleason's Gym (www.gleasonsgym.com), and in the UK, see Ultra White Collar Boxing (www.ultrawhitecollarboxing.co.uk), with over 100 locations in the United Kingdom.
2 Data taken from *Statista* (2021).
3 Data taken from www.boxrec.com.

4 And in fact a Muay Thai-themed fitness boxing gym has now opened in the West Bottoms, only a few blocks from Authentic Boxing.
5 For two poignant filmic glimpses of Frazier's post-boxing life at the gym—and intimate views of the 3rd floor apartment—see Dower (2008) and Todd (2011).

References

Boxrec.com. 2021. Accessed 15 June 2021. https://boxrec.com/en/locations/people?&offset=3200

Dower, John. 2008. *Thrilla in Manila*. Darlow Smith Productions.

Statista. 2021. Accessed 15 June 2021. https://www.statista.com/statistics/756773/boxing-for-fitness-participants-us

Todd, Mike. 2011. *Joe Frazier: When the Smoke Clears*. Riverhorse Productions.

US Census. 2020. Accessed 15 June 2021. https://www.census.gov

Part II
Boxing and philosophy

6 Outline of a constraint theory of sport

Among the many themes to have emerged from the foregoing discussion of boxing and urban culture one stands out prominently—namely, the effects that various forms of structural and physical violence can and do have on those pro boxers who reside in marginalized sectors of America's cities. Mechanisms of oppression, be they ethnoracial or neoliberal, place severe limitations on the choices and courses of action of those who inhabit such locations. At the cultural level individuals are drawn to the sport of boxing because it provides an alternate framework for them to electively pursue status, respect, and self-mastery in contexts structured by forces of depredation, disrespect, and domination. Culturally speaking, in choosing to become a boxer one does not merely become an athlete. Rather, one elects to fashion an identity *qua boxer* in contexts where most, if not all, other constraints are structurally and oppressively imposed from without. Hence, it was argued that in urban cultural terms being a boxer means far more than being an athlete; it means persistently choosing, in the face of structural obstacles, to strive to achieve a unique form of self-mastery in and through boxing.

But competitive pugilism is not only about self-mastery and the pursuit of relative autonomy—though it may be primarily about that for many urban-based professional boxers in the United States. Boxing is a cultural practice, to be sure, but it is also a formalized and institutionalized sport that entails individual rationality, creativity, and striving to excel in training and actual competition. Thus, in what follows I want to connect the complex dynamics of boxing and culture more broadly to a philosophical account of *competitive* sport and, specifically, the constraints that define and enable violent combat sport competition in boxing.[1] Indeed, the core philosophical argument of this chapter is that engagement in all competitive sports—from boxing

DOI: 10.4324/9781003196693-6

to bowling to badminton—is to a greater or lesser degree shaped by the interaction of three kinds of constraints.

The first, as we have seen in the case of boxing, are given or structural constraints—be they ethnoracial, economic, or even geographical—that characteristically delimit individuals' sport of choice. For it is no accident or quirk of individual preference that athletes who choose to compete as NASCAR drivers do not typically also consider a career in pro boxing—or vice versa; and it seems obvious that residents of Honolulu are geographically constrained in ways that favor the pursuit of competitive surfboarding over, say, bobsledding or luge. The second is, then, choice of constraints—for while structural constraints narrow what sport is feasible and 'makes sense' for a given individual, they do not singularly determine which particular sport should be pursued. All other things being equal, athletes who seek *competitive* edge will rationally opt for the sport to which they have structural access, elective affinities (such as a certain relationship to violence, as we saw in the case of boxing; or, say, familiarity with livestock, in the case of bull-riding), and in which they are most likely to excel. The third kind of constraint, as we shall see, entails individual choices *within* elective constraints that maximize skill and creativity—how one plays the game of one's choosing, as it were.

Now, the philosophical scaffolding for the kind of embedded rationality in competitive sport that I want to elaborate here can be found in the constraint theory of Jon Elster. Indeed, though Elster's work has not yet made its way into the philosophy of sport, the purpose of this chapter is to outline a novel theory of sport based loosely on his work—what I shall call a 'constraint theory of sport'. In the most general of terms, constraint theory is Jon Elster's unique attempt to develop a conception of rational action that is thick enough to capture the relationship between limits on human action (given constraints or structures) and the choices that can and cannot be made when individuals are embedded within such limits (preferences and courses of action). Although it has many dimensions and applications, the seeds of constraint theory can be found in Elster's *Ulysses and the Sirens* (1984), where he argues that all human action is the result of two successive filtering devices:

> The first is defined by the set of structural constraints, which cuts down the set of abstractly possible courses of action and reduces it to the vastly smaller subset of feasible actions. The second filtering process is the mechanism that singles out which member of the feasible set shall be realized. (Elster 1984, 113)

What makes Elster's thinking pertinent here is that he is interested in not merely the rationality of individual preferences and choice-maximizing action but also: (a) the role that structural constraints play in shaping those preferences and choices; (b) the fact that constraints on human action are not deterministic but can themselves be reflexively selected by individuals; and (c) the forms of choice and action, such as creative and skillful action, wherein these filters are not successive but interactive.

Now, the mythological hero Ulysses is Elster's model of a constraint theorist in action. For in his encounter with the Sirens, structural constraints (technological limits that require Ulysses travel by boat and not, say, airplane or helicopter; or the absence of long-distance electronic listening devices) and elective constraints (stopping up his rowers' ears and having himself lashed to the mast of the ship) interact and creatively enable what would have otherwise been an impossible course of action. Put in Elsterian terms, structural (given) constraints embed but do merely determine Ulysses' rational pursuit here; indeed, his creative choice of constraints frees him to safely hear the call of the Sirens (a choice within and enabled by those very constraints).

In Elster's more recent study, *Ulysses Unbound* (2000), he shifts his attention away from structural constraints in an attempt to characterize more fully the interaction of individual choices of constraints and choices within constraints in an analysis of creativity and constraints in the arts, where artists bind (and often seek to unbind) themselves in various ways. In this study as well, Elster provocatively suggests but does not develop the relevance of constraint theory for the philosophy of sport (Elster 2000, 281). Thus, let me briefly summarize Elster's thinking about art, before extending that thinking broadly to sport and then, more narrowly, to boxing.

In his constraint–theoretical account of art, Elster argues that artistic creation is 'guided by the aim of maximizing aesthetic value under constraints' (Elster 2000, 200). In art, according to Elster, constraints are not so much objectively given or 'hard' but rather 'soft' constraints or conventions—those 'restrictions that constitute a specific genre' (Elster 2000, 190), as Elster says. On Elster's account, the soft constraints or conventions in the arts are best understood as constitutive rules. Adhering to them, like adhering to the rules of chess, does not merely normatively regulate artistic endeavors; it defines such behavior as a *specific kind* of *artistic* endeavor. Yet, Elster is no mere formalist. His analysis concedes that sonnet writers, if they are to be skilled composers who achieve anything of aesthetic value or excellence, cannot simply adhere to or unthinkingly embody their chosen constraints.

Following the rules is simply not enough: the point of writing a sonnet, Elster suggests, is to write one well or in a maximally excellent way *within* the binding constraints of sonnet-writing.[2]

In many respects, such is the case, or so I want to argue, with competitive athletes as well. They, too, are engaged in a more or less complex practice aimed at constitutively constrained maximization. In competing in a particular sport, athletes, like artists, have, from within a context of pre-filtered and pre-filtering structural constraints, deliberately adopted the constitutive rules of a specific sport. Opting to be bound by the rules of tennis is what in one sense it means to play tennis and be a tennis player. Of course, *how* one plays and competes—the quality of the choices and the skillfulness and creativity of the moves one makes—within those binds/rules of tennis is what lends excellence to tennis playing and makes one a better or worse tennis player. In this regard, we might say Roger Federer is Shakespearean in his athletic realization of constrained maximization in the sport of tennis.

The basic Elsterian argument by analogy being introduced here is that, at least at one level, all competitive sports are athletic genres in which individuals, embedded in various interactive constraints, strive to achieve constrained maximization. The inverse of such a striving would be something like engaging in sport (or art) as a leisure activity or recreational hobby where the only objective would be something akin to 'constrained diversion'. Drawing a distinction between the attitude of constrained maximization and that of constrained diversion does not necessarily imply that there are any essential differences between a competitive athlete and a recreational player, or between athletic action and mere play.

Instead, from the embedded rational-choice perspective I am developing here, such a distinction simply makes explicit the relative potential for increasing constitutive skill and creativity in each case. Like the accomplished sonneteer, the competitive athlete's committed maximizing orientation toward the constitutive rules of his or her sport characteristically enables skill levels and forms of creative action that are difficult if not impossible to realize in the pleasure-maximizing activity of constrained diversion. In contrast to constrained diversion, wherein any idiosyncratic number and type of constraints will do, in competitive athletics less is more for the sake of excellence: constraints that bind ('less') are adhered to explicitly for the purposes of achievement of excellence in skill and creativity ('more') within those constraints.

There is, to be sure, no need to push this rough analogy between constrained maximization in art and constrained maximization in sport too far. Important distinctions can and should be preserved.

The orientation athletes adopt in relation to the rules of their chosen sport is not identical to that of artists in relation to the conventions of their chosen genre. Artists often self-consciously seek to violate or reject the conventions of their genre by subverting or exceeding them. This is evident in much contemporary art. Competitive athletes, by contrast, must endeavor to maximize their creativity and constitutive skill levels within existing constitutive constraints.[3] The relative constitutive quality of constraints/rules in competitive sport, on the one hand, and conventions in art, on the other hand, are also quite different. While we might view the recent history of postmodern art, literature, and theatre as having eliminated (or exceeded) all conventions, there is a reason we do not have a similar vocabulary for 'postmodern sport'. Though it often seems that anything goes in postmodern poetry, what counts as playing tennis remains playing by the rules that constitute tennis (even if/when those rules are modified). And what counts as playing excellent tennis remains an individual's athletic ability to maximize his or her tennis-playing constitutive skills and creativity in the course of an actual tennis match.

The general point to be drawn from this difference in the nature of constraints in sports and the arts is that the relationship between constitutive rules and constitutive skills and creativity appears to be decisive for competitive sport in ways that it is not for art (or play). What introducing constraint theory to sport makes explicit is that in competitive sport constitutive rules are determinative for enabling the pursuit of constrained maximization of skill and creativity. The quantity and quality of constitutive skills to be maximized are dependent upon the quantity and quality of constitutive rules that enable (or disable) such maximization.

To put the matter in the terms of constraint theory, where a certain number of the right kinds of constraints obtain, more possibilities to achieve constitutively skilled excellence exist. Of course, what makes for the 'right kinds of constraints' in competitive sport is an essential, if open, normative question. This is especially the case in combat sport, which, unlike many other sports, is constituted by violent skills that, improperly constrained, not only risk the safety of the athletic participants but also threaten to undermine the activity *qua* sport—a point we shall return to in greater detail in the next chapter.

The kind of culturally informed rational choice approach to the theory of competitive sport I am proposing here shares certain features with two core elements of game playing identified by Bernard Suits (1995) in his 'The Elements of Sport'. Specifically, constraint theory shares with Suits a conception of the rules of sport as constitutive rules.

It also shares with Suits a general sense that game playing entails that game players adopt a certain attitude *as game players* toward those rules—or what Suits richly describes as 'the lusory attitude'. Athletes can be defined, at least in part, as individuals who take up a lusory attitude vis-à-vis constitutive rules: they choose their constraints or knowingly adopt constitutive rules 'just so the activity made possible by such acceptance can occur' (Suits 1995, 11).

Yet unlike Suits, and consistent with a culturally informed version of what in the philosophy of sport is called 'broad internalism', constraint theory aims to address the nature and effects of structural or given constraints; it also focuses on the normative importance of getting the constitutive constraints of sport right for the purpose of excellence and safety in competition.[4] To put the matter succinctly, while Suits makes clear that his object 'is to define *not well-played games*, but games' (Suits 1995, 10, emphasis added), a constraint theory of competitive sport seeks to analyze how and why and the extent to which competitions are (or are not) in fact 'well-played'. A constraint theory of competitive sport thus contains a critical supplement to Suits' formalist thinking. The argument could be summarized as follows: (a) competitive sport is ineluctably embedded in structural constraints; and (b) individual choices of constraints (electing to adopt the particular lusory attitude requisite for engagement in a given sport) should not merely make competition possible but also—and especially in combat sports—make for good and safe competition by enabling choices within those constraints that maximize constitutive skills and creativity and minimize risk of undue physical harm.

Put differently, a constraint theory of sport is intended to be both descriptive *and* normative. It is an attempt to scrutinize the complex ways in which the constitutive rules of sport make for more or less creative, skill-maximized, and safe sporting competitions. As we shall see in the next chapter, a constraint theory of sport's applied focus provides a critical analytic tool with which to understand and argue for modifications to the constitutive rules that define and enable a perilous sport like boxing. For boxing is not only a *culturally* sweet science of self-mastery; it is also a *rationally* sweet—and, indeed, bittersweet—science of constrained violent skill maximization.

Notes

1 I emphasize *competitive* here. Of course, as we saw in the case of Authentic Boxing, for many pro boxers the sport is far less about achieving competitive excellence than it is about 'being a boxer' in a certain milieu; this fact

highlights the sense in which boxing is a cultural practice. It is with the understanding that boxing is an embedded cultural practice that this section is devoted to theorizing boxing as a competitive professional sport.

2 To be sure, in the history of art, there are numerous exceptions to Elster's generalization about the pursuit of excellence within binding constraints. In fact, self-consciously violating the rules of sonnet-making, for example, is a way to play, as it were, with existing constraints in an effort to expand (or reject) what counts as excellence in sonneteering. I address this point—and contrast it with the pursuit of excellence in competitive athletics—briefly in what follows.

3 Of course there would appear to be obvious exceptions to this generalization. Consider snowboarding, wherein a new athletic genre—a new set of constitutive constraints—emerges. But such an exception, which is itself parasitic on existing constraints, only highlights the extent to which the pursuit of excellence in competitive sport—even new and hybrid sports—remains necessarily embedded within constitutive constraints of one sort or another.

4 For clear and to my mind compelling accounts of broad internalism in the philosophy of sport, see especially Russell (1999) and Simon (2014).

References

Elster, Jon. 1984. *Ulysses and the Sirens*. Cambridge: Cambridge University Press.

Elster, Jon. 2000. *Ulysses Unbound: Studies in Rationality, Precommitment, and Constraints*. Cambridge: Cambridge University Press.

Russell, John. 1999. 'Are Rules All an Umpire Has to Work With?' *Journal of the Philosophy of Sport* 26 (1): 27–49.

Simon, Robert L. 2014. 'Theories of Sport.' In *The Bloomsbury Companion to the Philosophy of Sport*, edited by Cesar R. Torres, 83–97. London: Bloomsbury.

Suits, Bernard. 1995. 'The Elements of Sport.' In *Philosophic Inquiry in Sport*, 2nd Edition, edited by William J. Morgan and Klaus V. Meier, 8–15. Champaign, IL: Human Kinetics.

7 Boxing as the bittersweet science of constraints

Among the normative advantages of the introduction of constraint theory to boxing, two are especially worth highlighting. First, with its insistence on how structural constraints embed but do not singularly determine rational choices, constraint theory eschews more paternalistic and deterministic accounts of the sport that imply boxers are merely the effects of various macro-level forces that 'push' them into pugilism. As we have seen, striving to become a boxer in the face of structural violence entails a daily commitment to self-mastery and relative autonomy vis-à-vis mechanisms of oppression. Qua agents, pro boxers in the United States are not reducible to mere functions of the structural constraints of the 'hood' any more than competitive fencers are reducible to the by-products of a privileged elite and primarily East Coast suburban milieu. In each case, what we see, from the standpoint of a constraint theory of sport, are athletes whose feasible choice of constraints (options to adhere to and compete within the constitutive rules of a particular sport) is embedded (albeit profoundly unequally and with highly divergent consequences) in given sets of structural constraints.

Second, a constraint theoretical account of a sport like boxing casts a critical light on how constitutive rules work—and, as we shall see, fail to work—to foster competitive excellence in the sport, which, like all combat sports, must continually seek to balance competitive excellence and constrained but skilled violence with the need to maintain relative safety for its competitors. A constraint theory of boxing allows us to focus simultaneously on the elusiveness of maintaining precisely this balance: how best to understand and maximize constitutive violent skills and creativity in pursuit of excellence in competitive combat and yet at the same time minimize the risks of physical harm in the course of such a pursuit. As it happens, professional boxing does not manage this balancing act particularly well. Indeed, from the standpoint of a

DOI: 10.4324/9781003196693-7

constraint theory of sport, what makes boxing a *bittersweet* science is not violence or risk of injury as such—one could say this about many sports—but rather the failure of boxing to achieve what Elster calls an 'optimal tightness of the bounds' (2000, 281).[1] In this chapter, then, I want, in a critical vein, to elaborate a constraint theory of boxing's 'suboptimal tightness' and suggest much-needed practical modifications to the constitutive rules of the sport.

Admittedly, from a distance, combat sport in general—and the sport of professional boxing in particular—would appear an unlikely candidate for constraint theorizing. Indeed, pugilism typically conjures up images of human action far more Hobbesian than Elsterian. From the outside looking in, boxing appears to be not a sport of rationally constrained maximization but rather an unbound state of nature. The boxing ring is frequently alluded to as a kind of observable site of raw egoism in which the virtues of force and fraud and the war of all against all appear in miniaturized form.

Sports announcers, popular media, and often boxers themselves do much to provoke this 'anything goes' image of the sport. Ringside commentators and 'experts' commonly describe professional boxing matches as 'street fights' or 'brawls', and boxers as 'street fighters' or 'brawlers'. As is well-known, the 1974 heavyweight championship fight in Zaire between Muhammad Ali and George Foreman was called the 'Rumble in the Jungle'; an episode of the popular American television series, *CSI*, opens with a boxing ring as a crime scene in which a professional boxer has been murdered in the course of a bout; and the popular *Rocky* film series presents the ring death of one of its lead protagonists as nothing less than a murder to be avenged in a future match. To this short list, we could easily add Mike Tyson's (and others') wild ring antics or the desire that 'Iron Mike' once expressed at a prefight press conference to eat the children of heavyweight champion Lennox Lewis.

The apparent irrationality and viciousness of boxing (and of some high-profile boxers) is surely conjured in such images, colorful language, and sound bites. Yet this tells us little about the *sport* of boxing, which is not reducible to 'fighting', *tout court*. Rumbles and street fights are forms of human action by definition *devoid* of rationally chosen constraints. Individuals engaged in such actions are limited only by the arbitrary motivations of their own emotions, the emotions or threats of others, circumstances, or some combination thereof. In an Elsterian sense, rumbles and street fights are paradigmatic of rationally unbound action. They lack, precisely, the bounds of rational choices designed to maximize creativity and skill that define and make possible athletic endeavors as such.

In dedicating themselves to the sport of boxing, by contrast, individuals seek to restrict choice in ways that enable creativity and skill maximization in competitive combat. The fact that in so many professional matches individual boxers fail to achieve constrained maximization and sustain what, later in life, will prove to be long-term cognitive injuries, is not the result of an absence of constraints. Instead, these are primarily the result of the suboptimal constraints constitutive of pro boxing. Indeed, to see why professional boxing suffers from suboptimal constraints we need only to contrast it with amateur boxing.

Amateur boxing is tightly classified by weight, age, and experience. Amateur boxers compete in single elimination tournaments and are seeded and compete only within designated age/weight/experience classifications. Round and bout lengths vary by classifications but are exceptionally brief in all cases: three three-minute rounds and one-minute rests between rounds for Elite and Senior male boxers (ages 19–40); four two-minute rounds and one-minute rests between rounds for Elite (ages 19–40) and Youth (17–18) female boxers; and three two-minute rounds for Junior (ages 15–16) and Novice (boxers who have competed in 10 or less sanctioned matches).[2]

Moreover, amateur bouts emphasize scoring by cleanly landed punches. Thus amateur bouts, with the short length of each round and overall compactness of the bouts (nine minutes total for Elite and Senior male boxers), characteristically feature high volume punching over power punching. Along with the number of quality punches landed in the target area, domination of bout via technical/tactical superiority and competitiveness are to be evaluated by five judges working independently of one another. Rounds are scored individually on a '10 point' must system, with 10 points mandatorily given to the winner of the round (the boxer who lands the highest number of quality punches, dominates via superior technical skills, and remains competitive) and 9 points given to the loser of the round in cases where the round has been very close; a 10–8 score is awarded where there is a clear winner to the round; and 10–7 (the lowest score) given when one boxer exhibits complete dominance over the other. A punch that knocks down an opponent is not weighted more than any other scoring punch. But clean landing body punches, though not always easy for judges to observe, are to be weighted over simple jabs. A standing '8-count'—a referee's decision to pause the bout for eight seconds to evaluate a boxer who may or may not have been knocked down—is not an automatic point deduction and only factors in a judge's evaluation if the '8-count' is used because the boxer is being dominated by his/her opponent. A referee may end the bout due to injury, one-sidedness, or inactivity (on the part of one or both boxers). To be sure, this is not an exhaustive list. But already we can see that the constitutive constraints of amateur boxing competitions are exceptionally tight, and clearly aim to foster a kind of excellence that places a premium on skills, creativity and optimizing *mutual engagement* over defensive strategies, stalling, and a reliance on single knockdown punches and heavy knockout-style head strikes. Moreover, with its narrow bands of classifications (age, weight, experience), elimination tournament-style matchmaking, compressed round and bout lengths, and emphasis on the number of quality blows landed, amateur boxing goes some way, however imperfectly, to minimizing risk of concussive head injury.[3]

All this is something that surely cannot be said of professional boxing. To begin with, pro boxers are classified only by weight. Age and experience do not constrain matchmaking in pro boxing. One can 'go pro' at age 18 in the United States (15 years of age in Mexico) without having had *any* amateur experience, and there is no upper age limit on who can box professionally. Though an issue we shall address in a subsequent chapter, here we must point out that, unlike amateur boxing, matchmaking in professional boxing is a morally fraught enterprise in which promoters and trainers play a heavy hand in determining matchups primarily designed to further the career of one boxer largely at the expense of his or her counterpart. In fact, much of pro boxing features intentionally one-sided pairings in which, for example, individuals with no amateur experience, or boxers 'faded' or 'shopworn' from too many fights and/or too many years in the sport, are matched against rising prospects with extensive amateur experience. Indeed, matchmaking in professional boxing often amounts to little more than arranging bouts between boxers and the 'opponents' (club fighters, trial horses, and journeymen, as they are derogatively known in pro boxing) preselected for them to defeat.

And unlike amateur boxing, pro bouts are much longer—12 rounds for championship fights and anywhere from 4–10 rounds for regional pro competitions. Moreover, regardless of the overall length of the bout or weight or experience or age of the fighters, in pro boxing round length is standardized to three minutes per round (2 for professional female boxers), with one minute rest periods between each round.

Like amateur boxing, pro bouts are also scored by rounds using the '10 point' must system—yet at the professional level judges typically weigh 'effective aggression' and heavy (power) punches that 'do damage' over cleanly landed blows that do not. The pro boxer who wins the round must be awarded 10 points, as in amateur boxing, and the loser, assuming he or she has not been knocked down, is awarded 9 points. In pro boxing, however, knockdowns are weighted and scored by subtracting a point for the downed competitor. Thus, a round that includes a knockdown is scored 10–8, and a round that includes two knockdowns is scored 10–7. Further, professional boxing matches are not ended by the referee due to deliberate inactivity. On the contrary, and given the length of the bouts, it is not uncommon for a professional boxer to intentionally 'give away rounds'—often many or even most rounds—and turn himself into a human punching bag with an eye toward letting his counterpart 'punch himself out' and then, in a kind of dramatic come-from-behind 'lottery moment' seek to land a knockout punch much later in the fight.

Perhaps the most famous example of this is evident in the so-called 'rope-a-dope' method invented and popularized by Muhammad Ali during the middle and late years of his professional career when his skills began to diminish. In adopting such a purely defensive posture, a boxer leans against the ropes with guard held high, enduring blow after blow (often but not always fully blocked) as he gives away rounds in hopes that his opponent will eventually exhaust himself and become easy prey to a knockout punch in later rounds. As it did for Ali, this approach proves at times to be a way to win professional boxing matches—especially for boxers with a 'thick coat' (i.e., those who can take a beating) and/or 'heavy hands' (i.e., those who can punch exceptionally hard).

Yet it does so only at the cost of skill and creativity maximization in the ring and, thus, tends to undermine excellence in competitive pugilistic combat. Put differently, it makes the fight athletically inferior, stylistically ugly, and far more dangerous; indeed, the frequent adoption of stalling tactics in pursuit of a late round knockout in boxing demonstrates how pro boxing's suboptimal constraints enable a perilous form of de-skilled, artless, and self-endangering inaction. The boxer who turns himself into a punching bag for most of the match exponentially endangers his own well-being over the course of the bout and his career. As Ali's post-boxing career—and the fate of many other boxers at much lower levels who adopt similar strategies in the ring—makes painfully clear, the length of bouts (15 rounds in Ali's day), scoring premium placed on knockdowns and knockouts, and non-penalization of deliberate inactivity combine to greatly enhance the risk of long-term concussive head injury.

To clarify further how and why suboptimal constraints can so adversely affect competitive sport, we may consider the following counterfactual example. Imagine that competitive singles tennis contained, as pro boxing does, a knockout 'lottery moment' in which a player, no matter how far behind in a match, could be declared the winner if she is able to land, say, an un-returnable shot in bounds at a speed of 100 or more miles per hour. In such a case, we would say that competitive excellence (skill and creativity) is fundamentally diminished not merely as a result of athletes' choices within constraints (how they play the game) but rather the problematic effect of the existing suboptimal tightness of the constitutive bounds that define and (dis) able their competition.

From the critical perspective of a constraint theoretical account of professional boxing, then, the constitutive rules of the sport are in need of optimization—for reasons of maximizing competition and, indeed, minimizing risk of concussive head injury. Clearly, the length of fights should be shortened. The standard 12 round championship fight is simply too long. And when combined with a scoring system that places a premium on knockdowns and allows for a knockout punch 'lottery moment' victory, 12 round bouts enable and even encourage inactive and artless 'competitions' that put boxers at increased risk for the kind of sustained concussive blows to the head that have severe long-term health consequences. In the interest of both constrained maximization and head injury minimization, 8 round bouts with a scoring system that mirrors that of amateur boxing are warranted.

While condensing the length of matches and shifting the emphasis away from aggressive power punching and the over-weighting of knockdowns are key to ensuring competitive excellence and a modicum of safety in the sport, deliberate inactivity must also be penalized. With the exception of a 'feeling out' period in the first round, a minimum number of attempted punches per round should be established—with offenders penalized 1 point for failing to meet that minimum. Flush strikes to the head of each boxer should be counted, and an upper allowable limit on the number of clean head punches per fight established.[4] Once that threshold is crossed, the bout should be stopped and a boxer would be said to lose on 'head punches', in much the same way that he could lose 'on cuts'.[5] The technology needed to track a minimum number of punches thrown per round, as well as total blows landed to the head, is currently in use in most high level professional bouts. Known as CompuBox™, this blow-scoring system is operated by individuals who electronically key in punches by accuracy (thrown or landed), location (head or body), and type (jab or power shot). In this way, actual data regarding punches thrown and landed in a pro fight is already available and could easily be used to penalize deliberate inactivity or stop a fight due to excessive head strikes.

In terms of enhancing competition and diminishing injury, the advantages of such constitutive rule modifications would not be insignificant. Shortening bouts, using amateur scoring, and establishing a minimum number of punches thrown per round would encourage active and mutually engaged combat (competition rather than a prolonged workout on a human heavy bag) and thus help to discourage versions of the 'rope-a-dope' and stalling in pursuit of a come-from-behind victory via knockout. Real-time data regarding blows to the head would provide an empirical basis for fight stoppages for health and safety reasons. Moreover, in a sport where refusing to continue and 'quitting on the stool' can mean the end of a career, it would take the decision to end the bout out of the hands of a boxer's cornerman—a ringside coach who, on any given night, has a vested but deeply conflicted interest in the health and relative success of his or her boxer.[6]

This chapter has sought to apply constraint theory in a critical analysis of professional boxing. The basic argument has been that it is not individual irrationality or simply the determining power of structural constraints but, rather, a failure to optimize the bounds—or constitutive constraints—of the sport that plagues professional pugilism. A constraint theory of pro boxing helps to make explicit the 'bitterness', as it were, of the 'sweet science' in ways more functionalist and paternalistic treatments of the sport tend to obscure. Such a critical approach also allows us to offer practical alternatives—however provisional and in need of further refinement—for reforming some of the many suboptimal constraints that currently hamper this violent sport. For the normative problem with pro boxing is not the questionable existence of pugilism as a sport. Paternalistic calls to ban professional boxing are misplaced and would be better directed toward reformation of the constitutive rules that so poorly define the sport. Constraint theory aims to do precisely that. It provides us with a rich normative framework for criticizing—and transforming—the bittersweet science in ways that are likely to enhance the potential for skill and creativity and diminish the risks of concussive head injury in competition.

Notes

1 Or, to paraphrase Russell (1999), the normative argument here is that the constitutive rules of professional boxing often undermine, rather than maintain and foster, the excellences embodied in achieving the lusory goal of the sport.

2 There are other classifications, to be sure; in the interest of space this list of classifications is meant to be representative only.
3 With shorter bouts, longer rests between bouts, and emphasis on skilled creativity and diversity of striking types and target zones, Muay Thai (the 'art of eight limbs') would also seem to accomplish much of the same.
4 In contrast to Dixon (2001) and his call to ban blows to the head, which merely introduces yet another set of suboptimal—in this case overly tight—constraints to the sport of boxing. Banning head strikes would foster matches in which excellence in boxing—complex punch combinations, ring generalship, feints, and slipping punches, among many other things—would be replaced with plodding 'rope-a-dope' styles that need protect only the body, as well bouts with few cleanly landed body blows. The reason for this, as boxers know, is obvious: the most effective way to land body punches in boxing is to *combine them with punches to the head*.
5 The precise number of maximum head punches that leads to a defeat is, to be sure, debatable, and would surely vary based on a variety of factors (age, length of fight, or, potentially, number of previous fights for each boxer) and hence a topic to be determined and continually reviewed by sanctioning bodies and medical experts.
6 A point we shall return to in chapter 10.

References

Dixon, Nicholas. 2001. 'Boxing, Paternalism, and Legal Moralism.' *Social Theory and Practice* 27 (2): 323–344.
Elster, Jon. 2000. *Ulysses Unbound: Studies in Rationality, Precommitment, and Constraints*. Cambridge: Cambridge University Press.
Russell, John. 1999. 'Are Rules All an Umpire Has to Work With?' *Journal of the Philosophy of Sport* 26 (1): 27–49.

8 Combat sport violence and sparring

Boxing, especially professional boxing, is a most dangerous sport, its perilousness exacerbated by suboptimal constitutive rules, as we have seen. Nevertheless, however poorly constituted, part of the value of participation in such a dangerous sport surely lies, as Russell (2005) argues, in the many ways it poses 'a challenge to capacities for judgment and choice that involves all of ourselves—our body, will, emotions, and ingenuity—under conditions of physical duress and danger *at the limits of our being*' (14). In fact, at the cultural level, becoming a boxer is a way to electively impose limits on one's 'being' and strive to achieve status, respect, and self-mastery in difficult urban contexts, as we saw previously. But boxing is not simply a dangerous sport, it is a profoundly violent one. And yet the nature and function of the violence peculiar to boxing—and combat sport more generally—is not well understood. Simon (2001) points out that boxing 'makes violent central' (355).[1] Here we must go further and emphasize that violence is not merely central but rather *essential* to the sport. Thus, boxing should be distinguished from other dangerous but non-violent sports. For while not all dangerous sports are violent (e.g., mountain climbing or ski jumping), all violent sports (e.g., boxing or Mixed Martial Arts) are dangerous. Indeed, unlike mountain climbing or ski jumping, a sport such as boxing is constituted not merely through endangering one's own being but also via the violent endangerment of another human being through physical (fistic) contestation. Hence in terms of danger and violence, it could be argued that all competitive combat sport should be understood as mutual endangerment in and only in skilled violence inflicted on another human being. As the saying goes in boxing, 'they call it a fight for a reason'.

In this chapter, then, I want to move in a related but different direction regarding the questions of violence and values in sport. Rather than a consideration of the value of a dangerous sport such as boxing,

DOI: 10.4324/9781003196693-8

Combat sport violence and sparring 67

the focus here is on exploring the violence peculiar to combat sport competition and training. Put differently, it is not merely the value of dangerous sport but also the nature and function of violence that must be clarified in the case of boxing and other combat sports.

To that end, and in addition to the discussion of structural violence developed earlier, I want to establish a distinction between violence, on the one hand, and two types of sport violence, on the other hand. Specifically, I shall argue that, adequately understood, *combat sport violence is constitutively skilled violence*.[2] There is indeed, as Russell (2005) rightly maintains, value to the ways that the use of such skilled violence in mutually endangering contests tests human limits and fortitude. But that is not my primary focus in what follows. Instead, I shall suggest that the deeper value of combat sport is found not in the ring but in the gym, in the most commonplace element of training unique to all combat sport, namely, that of sparring. In combat sport *sparring* skilled violence takes on a different form and function, and does not simply entail mutual endangerment (though it is of course dangerous) but more fundamentally *mutual betterment*. Indeed, if there is a deeper value to be found in the dangerous and violent sport of boxing (and, by extension, combat sport more generally), then it does not reside only—or even primarily—in the existential limit-testing of competition but rather in the cooperative ethos of sparring.

Though the notions are sometimes used interchangeably, violence and sport violence are clearly not identical. Indeed, the term 'violence', construed in the everyday sense of physical harm, characteristically denotes injurious actions limited and motivated solely by arbitrary and idiosyncratic factors, such as emotions, prejudices, threats, circumstances, and so on. Violence in this (non-sporting) sense is 'thin', and has nothing to do with sport (though, admittedly, it can and does happen in sport from time to time). That is to say that violence per se is little more than *unconstrained* assault. Violence in this regard would include activities like gang attacks, road rage incidents, random assaults, and bar brawls. Such 'anything goes' violent encounters are in fact paradigmatic of rationally unbound action—precisely the opposite of the account of sport as constrained maximization developed in the previous chapters.

By contrast, *sport violence*, broadly construed, would seem to take one of two forms. The first is that of violent action and behavior that transpire outside the constitutive rules of a sport and are an inessential but nevertheless generally accepted part of that sport. A paradigmatic example of this kind of sport violence is fighting in ice hockey. Though commonplace at professional levels of the sport, the playing of ice hockey matches is not defined and enabled by such behavior; indeed, pro ice hockey matches can be—and often are—played without any fighting.³ Fistic skills are not constitutive of ice hockey in any way. Yet the kind of fighting peculiar to ice hockey is not, like violence per se, a purely 'anything goes' proposition. Instead, it is governed by informal expectations operative within the sport itself: in a ritual familiar to all ice hockey fans, fights ensue when players square off with one another, drop their sticks and gloves, and in most cases seek to hold a counterpart with one hand while punching wildly to his head with the other hand.⁴ Striking with the stick or a gloved hand, kicking with sharp blades, eye-gouging, and so on are not acceptable forms of fighting in ice hockey—though of course all forms of fighting are against the rules in the sport. Let us call this kind of sport violence *associative sport violence*, insofar as it is, unlike violence per se, non-arbitrary and associated with but not constitutive of a particular sport.

The second form of sport violence entails action and behavior that necessarily transpires within and, indeed, constitutes a given sport. A boxing match, unlike an ice hockey match, is only possible in and through the punching of another human being. And competing in a boxing match is in its essence about seeking excellence and creativity in punching (and not getting punched). Let us call this *constitutive sport violence*. Constitutive sport violence is the ineliminable form of violence that necessarily defines and makes possible combat sports such as boxing. Combat sport violence must be distinguished from violence per se and associative sport violence, inasmuch as the latter two forms lack precisely the interaction of constitutive rules (constraints) and embedded and embodied individual choices and actions (pursued within those constraints) necessary to maximize athletic creativity and skill.⁵

Or, to put the matter in Suitsian terms, violence per se and associative sport violence lack robust forms of the lusory attitude. Combat sport violence, in contrast, is lusorily 'thick'; that is to say that combat sport violence is non-arbitrarily constituted by the adoption of shared binding constraints (rules) of the competition and the skillful and creative moves enabled by such constitutive constraints. In short, properly understood, the violence peculiar to a combat sport such as boxing is not violence per se or associative but rather *constitutively skilled violence*.

To capture the argument being made here we need only consider the difference among the skilled execution of a left jab–right cross–left hook combination in a boxing match, the throwing of a 'haymaker' punch in an ice hockey fight, and a bar brawl. Landing a complex

Combat sport violence and sparring 69

combination in boxing is a paradigmatic case of the thickness—the constitutively skilled quality—of violence in combat sport. Throwing a 'haymaker' in an ice hockey fight, while loosely bound by certain informal conventions, cannot be said to be a constitutive violent skill (though we can say that it is an associative violent skill). Meanwhile, a bar brawl 'haymaker' is pure violence and thus completely unbound. In other words: neither ice hockey fighting nor bar brawling can be said to contain constitutive skills precisely because there are no mutually binding constraints (and lusory attitudes) that *constitute* the activity of fighting in ice hockey or bar brawling *as sport*. Of course, one might be a 'good goon' in hockey or a 'successful' bar brawler in one's neighborhood, in the limited sense of having prevailed in numerous encounters, but that is itself an outcome in no way defined and made possible by the (non-existent) constitutive rules of fighting in ice hockey or brawling outside of a bar. In sum, the difference between violence per se and associative sport violence, on the one hand, and the kind of constitutive sport violence one finds in boxing, on the other hand, depends on the presence or absence of constitutive constraints and concomitant violent skills defined and enabled by those very constraints.

As we saw in the last chapter, the rules of pro boxing do not always optimize the constitutively skilled violence that defines and enables (and limits) what transpires in competitive boxing. Yet professional boxing, for all its faults, generally manages to preserve the core normative difference between violence and constitutive sport violence necessary to prevent it from lapsing into nothing more than unconstrained assault. Indeed, in pro boxing, the target striking area is tightly delimited; boxers are disqualified for striking a downed opponent; and a referee can make use of a mandatory eight count rule in which he evaluates a downed (or seemingly defenseless) fighter and gives him or her eight seconds to recover before deciding to continue or to stop the match.

By way of contrast, the same cannot be said of boxing's hybrid cousin, MMA. Indeed, MMA frequently vacillates between violence per se and constitutive sport violence. To see this one need look no further than the prominent role that boxing, Muay Thai and Jiu-Jitsu forms of combat play in MMA. As a hybrid sport that combines stand up and ground combat, it's no surprise that MMA athletes train extensively and seek to excel in boxing, Muay Thai and Jiu-Jitsu. Known as the 'art of eight limbs', Muay Thai entails stand up fighting constituted by the constrained use of fists, elbows, knees, and legs (shins). In consistently utilizing eight striking surfaces, it is far more physically devastating than mere Western style boxing or other Eastern martial arts, such as karate or judo. Thus, the constitutive rules of competitive Muay Thai include, among others, no striking when the opponent is down, no grappling, tackling, or choking, the mandatory use of specially padded gloves (6–10 ounces in weight, depending on the competitors' weight class), and 5-round matches consisting of three-minute rounds with two-minute rest periods between rounds.

But when introduced and practiced in the hybrid sport of MMA, the constitutive rules of boxing and Muay Thai proper largely melt away. MMA fighters do not wear boxing or Muay Thai gloves. Instead, they wear 4-ounce grappling (open-fingered) knuckle pads. Additionally, MMA rounds are five minutes in length, and offer competitors only a one-minute rest period between rounds. Championship MMA contests are mandatory (and non-title main event bouts are typically) 5-round fights—thus with rounds much longer than in boxing or Muay Thai contests.

The matter of MMA's violence is compounded with the widespread use of Jiu-Jitsu. The complex choke holds and python-like submission maneuvers of Jiu-Jitsu are designed to cut off the flow of oxygen and dislocate limbs. And while the constitutive rules of Jiu-Jitsu forbid striking of any kind (indeed, the penalty for striking in competitive Jiu-Jitsu is immediate disqualification), in MMA the sport is fused with boxing and Muay Thai in a way that makes certain combat sequences difficult to distinguish from an arbitrary 'anything goes' assault. In fact, MMA competitors are permitted to take down, mount, and repeatedly strike (with fists, elbows, and forearms, but not knees or feet) a downed (and often semi-conscious) opponent—a gruesome and assaultive practice known as 'ground and pound' that has no correlate in boxing or Muay Thai.

One often sees this in a three-phase combat sequence distinct to MMA. In the initial encounter, which begins with both fighters on their feet, boxing and Muay Thai style stand up fighting (punching and striking with fists, elbows, knees, and shins) leads to a knock down. In a furious second phase, the downed and semi-conscious fighter is mounted by his opponent and set upon with all manner of fists, elbows, and forearms—'ground and pound' moves, as noted above, which are *not* permitted in boxing, Muay Thai or Jiu-Jitsu—or any other combat sport, for that matter. In the final phase of the sequence, a bloodied and nearly defenseless man or woman is brutally choked unconscious or otherwise painfully submitted in a Jiu-Jitsu hold. In this kind of assailing sequence, the line between violence per se and the constitutive skilled violence of combat sport all but dissolves. In

MMA, unlike in boxing, constitutive sport violence often quickly degenerates into little more than a bar brawl pummeling. The 'thin' violence of unbound action—assault—overtakes the 'thick' combat sport violence of constitutively bound violent skills.

Yet a normative discussion of violence and sport violence in combat sports such as boxing and MMA should not be limited to what transpires in the course of competition. Fighters unlike, say, baseball or basketball players, do not have a designated 'pre-season' or an 'off-season', and hence train far more often than they actually compete. And there is in fact much violence—constitutively skilled violence—to be found in combat sport training, and, more specifically, in combat sport sparring. It, too, is constitutive and dangerous, but the constitutively skilled violence of sparring is designed and functions much differently than in actual competitions. For combat sport sparring requires mutual respect and prioritizes mutual betterment. Thus it is in sparring, I want to argue, that the deeper value of combat sport must be located. Indeed, if, as Simon et al. (2015) have claimed, sport competitions are about the 'mutually acceptable quest for excellence through challenge' (47), then combat sport sparring is surely about the mutually acceptable *quest for betterment through constitutively skilled violent cooperation*. In other words, as I hope to demonstrate in the remainder of this chapter, there is a kind of *moral mutualism* to be found in combat sport sparring.

With its rich potential for optimizing constraints, sparring is a crucial but rarely examined subgenre of boxing in which constitutive violent skills are used for the purpose of mutual betterment.[6] Though the value of sparring in boxing has hitherto eluded the philosophy of sport, the practice constitutes a normatively fertile subgenre of combat sport research, and merits further scrutiny. In-house sparring, in which athletes spar with other members of their gym or club, is a central part of the routine for all boxers (and in fact all competitive combat sport athletes). Professional boxers spar much more frequently than they compete. Sparring occupies a complex midpoint between training and an actual fight; moreover, it is far different from partner drills and pad work. And with its frequency (often twice per week), flexibility, and fluidity, sparring is not readily analogous to the occasional and characteristically halting 'scrimmage' or 'practice' match one finds in many other sports. Under the watchful eye of a good coach/trainer, in the continuous flow of an in-house spar diverse and emerging constraints and choices interact in ways explicitly intended to mutually expand and sharpen the constitutive violent skills possessed by *both* athletes.[7]

At their best, in-house sparring sessions become multi-layered and highly reflexive attempts at constrained maximization of skill and creativity tempered by and realized through the trainer's (and fighters') tightening (or loosening) the constraints of the spar. Individual boxers are obliged, deliberately, to reflexively incorporate modified or additional constraints—such as doubling up jabs or throwing only body shots for a set number of rounds—into their habits of athletic action. The ability (or inability) to do so in the course of a sparring session typically leads to the imposition of additional or different constraints by a coach/trainer in a fluid manner.

Moreover, the choice of a sparring counterpart is neither random nor preselected with the consent of the individual boxer but chosen instead by the coach/trainer based on boxers available on designated sparring days and the specific mutual objectives of the sparring session. In light of the immediate aim of mutual betterment rather than competitive excellence, pros and amateurs, women and men, heavyweights and middleweights can be paired without undermining the shared goal of skill improvement; indeed, under the trained eye of a good coach, such seemingly odd pairings can actually further enable the cultivation of skill and creativity among individual boxers.[8]

In sparring sessions, athletes 'fight' only in ways that are intended to instruct one another in mutually beneficial ways, such as when boxers reflexively 'correct' one another's mistakes with controlled well-placed blows. Sparring is pugilistic pedagogy in action. In contrast to the heat of competitions in the ring, sparring in the gym must be a mutually respectful and highly cooperative educational practice. Boxers who are not willing or able to orient themselves to the normative aims of mutual betterment—those who disrespect their partners by trying to 'get off' and land heavy blows in a sparring session—are in fact not allowed to continue to spar in a boxing gym.

In-house sparring, that is to say, is an example of moral mutualism in combat sport—it is a multi-layered and dynamic form of constitutively skilled violence whose end is mutual betterment. Put differently, in boxing, sparring entails mutually respectful and deeply reflexive social cooperation—it is a complex joint 'we' endeavor in *honing* constitutive violent skills and creativity *cooperatively*. Thus the value of sparring is not reducible to competitive ends—one doesn't 'win' or 'lose' an in-house spar, rather one cooperates, albeit violently, in the pursuit of mutual betterment. In contrast to competitive matches, in sparring constitutive skilled violence is doubly constrained—by the additional constraints of the spar (as imposed by the trainer/coach) and the fighters' shared commitment to mutual betterment, rather than victory.

To be sure, in boxing (and all combat sport) competitions one *fights* with an opponent. But in combat sport training/sparring one 'works', as the saying goes in the gym, with a *partner*. In-house sparring sessions are thus a unique form of 'co-labor' or 'team-work'; they are shared cooperative endeavors aimed at mutual enhancement in and through constitutively skilled violence. As such, in-house sparring cultivates a profoundly cooperative ethos that finds no easy analogy in other sporting forms of scrimmaging and practice matches. Hence, the value of an essentially violent sport such as boxing lies not—or, at the least, not only—in the competitive action of the ring but rather more fundamentally in the collaborative practices of the gym.

Notes

1 And for an extensive critique of the morally problematic character of boxing's violent 'ferocity' and 'viciousness', see especially Davis (1993).
2 Here my thinking is inspired by Torres (2000) and his illuminating account of 'constitutive skills'.
3 For an insightful critique of 'retaliatory violence', especially in ice hockey, see especially Dixon (2010). My interest here is not in a critique or defense of such violence, but rather to get a clearer conceptualization of the difference between violence and two kinds of sport violence (associative and constitutive).
4 For an extended discussion of ritualistic dimensions of sport violence, see Matthews and Channon (2017).
5 Of course that is not to say that ice hockey does not contain constitutive rules that define and enable skilled violence. A good hip-check in hockey, for example, is surely as skilled and creative (and as violent) as any left-hook to the body in boxing. But excellence in checking in hockey is a constitutively skilled form of violence *in the sport*, whereas throwing a left hook is not. And one could surely imagine playing the sport of ice hockey without checking—indeed, many youth leagues bar the practice—and still consider it hockey. But it is not clear how boxing could exist without punching and remain the sport of boxing. In other words, constitutively skilled violence may be part of many non-combat sports, but it is an essential and ineliminable feature of combat sport.
6 Dixon (2015) implicitly acknowledges a similar point when he admits that sparring in MMA would not be subject to his moral critique.
7 Of course in-house sparring sessions that take place in the lead up to a competitive match have a somewhat different air about them. Such sessions are characteristically more intense, and the aims and benefits of the spar are deliberately weighted on the side of the athlete who has an upcoming match. But even in such cases, the practice of sparring remains mutually (if not equally) beneficial and demands high levels of reflexive social cooperation and mutual respect to be effective. Perhaps the only case in which sparring may not entail reflexive social cooperation and mutual respect in the manner characterized here can be found at the more privileged economic levels of

professional combat sport, where training camps in preparation for a marquee fight have the budget to bring in paid sparring partners from another gym/club. In such cases, the sparring 'partner' becomes merely an *employee*.

8 In fact, during my time at Authentic Coach Edgar often had me spar younger and less experienced amateur youth boxers (ages 11–15 or so) while throwing only jabs from my knees. This gave the kids a chance to develop and land basic punch combinations and, needless to say, forced me to improve my defensive skills, such as maintaining a tight guard and maximizing head movement to slip punches.

References

Davis, Paul. 1993. 'Ethical Issues in Boxing.' *Journal of the Philosophy of Sport* 20 (1): 48–63.

Dixon, Nicholas. 2010. 'A Critique of Violent Retaliation in Sport.' *Journal of the Philosophy of Sport* 37 (1): 1–10.

Dixon, Nicholas. 2015. 'A Moral Critique of Mixed Martial Arts.' *Public Affairs Quarterly* 29 (4): 365–384.

Matthews, Christopher R. and Alex Channon. 2017. 'Understanding Sports Violence: Revisiting Foundational Explorations.' *Sport in Society* 20 (7): 751–767.

Russell, John. 2005. 'The Value of Dangerous Sport.' *Journal of the Philosophy of Sport* 32 (1): 1–19.

Simon, Robert. 2001. 'Violence in Sports.' In *Ethics in Sport*, 2nd Edition, edited by William J. Morgan, Klaus V. Meier, and Angela Schneider, 345–356. Champaign, IL: Human Kinetics.

Simon, Robert, Cesar Torres, and Peter Hager. 2015. *Fair Play: The Ethics of Sport*, 4th Edition. Boulder, CO: Westview Press.

Torres, Cesar. 2000. 'What Counts as Part of a Game?: A Look at Skills.' *Journal of the Philosophy of Sport* 27 (1): 81–92.

9 Fight plan aesthetics

The foregoing chapters in this section have sought to develop a novel theory of sport, and then to apply that theory in a critical analysis of boxing and, to a limited extent, combat sport more generally. What remains to be considered in this study are some of the aesthetic dimensions and normative complexities of what transpires in an actual professional boxing match. Thus, the focus of this chapter is the development and implementation of a 'fight plan' in boxing, while a critical discussion of the moral dilemmas of 'cornering' (coaching during a boxing match) is the explicit concern of the final chapter.

In order to capture what I shall call the 'fight plan aesthetics' and 'cornerman ethics' of boxing, we must direct our attention not only to the fight per se but also to the period between rounds of a professional boxing match. For boxing matches are often won or lost between rounds—in the sometimes calm but more often frantic periods during which the boxer returns to her or his corner and engages with a cornerman/coach. In such designated intervals—60 seconds every three minutes in professional boxing—the training, sparring, and strategy of six weeks, the interaction of coach and athlete, and the ebb and flow of the fight intersect in ways that are often decisive for the outcome of the match and, indeed, an athlete's career.

Inasmuch as the goal of a pro boxing match is to win, a good cornerman/coach and his boxer/athlete must execute a fight plan and at the same time jointly improvise and continually rewrite that plan between rounds as the story of the fight unfolds in real time. In view of the physical danger and need to mentally manage fear and pain, *winning the story of the fight* is essential to victory and a successful career in professional pugilism. Yet as Mike Tyson once remarked, everyone has a plan 'until they get punched in the mouth'. Thus, it would be more accurate to say that it is in the narrative or storyline a cornerman fashions between rounds for (and with) his boxer *after* the

DOI: 10.4324/9781003196693-9

latter is punched in the mouth that the fight is often won or lost. In boxing such between round narratives, if they are to be effective in the theatrical heat of the contest, cannot simply restate the fight plan or merely describe what transpired in the previous round. Rather, to be effective they must conceal, dissemble, and creatively (mis)represent with an eye toward crafting a winning narrative in the face of extreme adversity and significant physical risk.

How best to characterize philosophically this kind of athletic storytelling oriented not merely—or even primarily—toward a correct description of the facts of the match but rather a shared illusion of overcoming those facts? The dissimulating narratives that emerge between the rounds of a professional boxing match are not ones that easily align with any aesthetic notions of truth or beauty in the classical sense. Rather, to borrow a conception from Friedrich Nietzsche, the 'truths' of those between rounds narratives are better understood as the result of a 'moving army of metaphors, metonyms, and anthropomorphisms' (*ein bewegliches Heer von Metaphern, Metonymien, Anthropomorphismen*) produced by the 'art of dissimulation' (*Verstellungskunst*).[1] Thus, I want to claim here that the unorthodox 'aesthetics' of a boxing fight plan as it emerges between rounds is best characterized as a dissimulating narrative.[2] This kind of aesthetic orientation toward a sport such as boxing views combat as a theatrical contest to be won not merely through skill and forthrightness but also via will and dissimulation in the narrative flow of competition.[3] Of course, we should acknowledge at the outset that many, if not all, 'game plans' in sport competitions entail some degree of narrative. But professional boxing, as I hope to show, is surely the most acute—and one of the most morally fraught—of exercises in the art of dissimulative narration in competitive sport.

Discussions of the aesthetics of boxing typically focus on the social and cultural history of the sport, the craft and physical beauty of the boxer, or the embodied art of fighting.[4] While probing in their own right, as indicated above the present discussion is more narrowly intended. What is of interest in this chapter are fight plan narratives that emerge in the course of professional pugilistic *competition*—how and why and with what consequences, that is to say, fight plans are (re)fashioned in the dissimulating narratives emergent between rounds.

Yet to grasp adequately the significance of pugilistic fight planning, we must begin by understanding how such between round narratives are themselves shaped by and embedded in a set of pre-existing plot lines peculiar to the sport of boxing. Indeed, it would not be an overstatement to say that nearly every professional boxing match is framed by one of two pre-existing narratives. The first contains a commercially familiar plot line and occurs at the highest level, in the premier six and seven (and even eight) figure big-money fights that are globally televised and take place in Las Vegas, London, and other major capitals throughout the world. Here, the main storylines anticipate clashes between more or less equally matched elite boxers. The respective characters of the boxers are dramatized in ways that stereotype and often hyper-ethnicize them and their upcoming 'battle' in the ring. Hence, one hears about a 'slick', 'stylish', or 'brash' boxer (Arturo 'Thunder' Gatti) and the 'hard-working' puncher ('Irish' Mickey Ward). Such hyped and heavily marketed narratives are perhaps the ones most widely associated with pro boxing. But in fact, these remain the exception in the mundane and rather proletarian world of professional pugilism.

Indeed, the overwhelming number of professional matches is far more prosaic, far less lucrative, much lower profile and comes without any advertising or marketing budget. Such matches take place in local casinos, gymnasia, clubs, and even outdoor car parks, and are by design not all that competitive. And it is here that we see the second kind of ready-made narrative frame. The pre-existing narrative for these fights—informed by their lack of competitive character and impoverished purses—contains a carefully shaped storyline in which a 'boxer' is matched against an 'opponent' in a bout whose outcome is more or less determined in advance. To play the character of 'the boxer' in such a narrative is to be the fighter who is up-and-coming, typically younger, has a good win-loss record, and is in need of some competitive rounds but does not want to risk losing or injury. To play the character of 'the opponent', by contrast, is to inhabit a role that ranges from 'lamb to slaughter' to punching bag to game but hopeless underdog.

Regardless of which of these two framing narratives are at work in advance of a professional boxing match, from the perspective of the coach and athlete the central storyline in the theater of the ring—and in the actual drama of all combat sports—is about successfully imposing one's will through highly skilled but constrained and creative violence.[5] Indeed, as we saw in the previous chapter, professional boxing is a dangerous sport unlike most others insofar as it requires two individuals to engage in constitutively skilled violence—to struggle head-to-head to impose their will on one another through the violent but highly skilled and tightly constrained use of their fists.

The successful imposition of one's will through the maximization of constitutively skilled violence is what, in the end, wins a boxing match and makes one an excellent prize-fighter; athletically speaking, the dogged pursuit of such excellence in the gym and the ring is what makes a fighter a *boxer*. And in fact, even boxers who appear on a professional card as 'the opponent' in the pre-fight narrative are presented with an opportunity—however improbable and seemingly predetermined to the contrary—to rise to the occasion and impose their will and excellence in skilled violence in ways that win the fight. Such upsets do in fact happen from time to time even at the lowest levels of the sport, and it is precisely such a dramatic reversal of the pre-existing script that makes local and regional boxing scenes, despite their relatively modest levels of professionalism and skill, compelling for participants and audiences alike.

Embedded within these two pre-fight faming narratives, which designate individual boxers as either ethnoracial stereotypes in a kind of clash of cultures, or stock characters ('the boxer' or 'the opponent') in an athletic drama, is always a second, more specific script—a fight plan—and its revision in the course of the fight. Such individualized plans and their execution are a mix of strategies tailored to skills, and stories tailored to wills. In boxing, a good fight plan—like any good game plan—must be based on an athlete's strengths and his or her opponent's weaknesses, and yet be flexible enough to be improvised, even drastically altered, by coach and athlete in the heat of competition. Put most generally, a fight plan—like any athletic game plan—is ultimately a projected narrative of how the competition could unfold. Given the contingencies of athletic competition—in particular those of professional combat sport competitions, where last minute replacement competitors are not uncommon—the draft game plan must be open-ended enough to allow for drastic plot twists and concomitant dissimulative turns once the actual competition begins.

This is especially the case in professional boxing, where once the competition begins the fight plan is sketched and re-sketched in regular, if often nakedly frenzied, one-minute intervals of metaphoric embellishments and metonymic understatements between boxer and corner.[6] Thus, a corner may dissemblingly tell his boxer—often in colorful language laced with a mix of euphemisms, gym slang, and expletives—that he or she looks good or won the round, or that the opponent is tired or hurt—when in fact the opposite is the case. In a dissimulative set of responses, the boxer nods, says that he or she feels ok and is ready to go again, even after suffering round after round of brutal blows. What must be emphasized is that the accuracy of these emergent between rounds narratives is not debated, or even of primary concern to coach and athlete. But neither are such narratives wholly arbitrary or willy-nilly. Instead, the power of the improvised narrative generated by the corner and boxer resides in its *dissimulative force*—not in its correct representation of the facts but rather in its metaphoric and metonymic power to dissemble and craft a meaningful and relevant narrative of actualizing the will to win *despite those facts*. In the intervals between rounds, that is to say, it is the power of the art of dissimulation to disclose possible ways for the boxer to impose his or her will—even when the risk and danger in seeking to do so is greatest.

Professional boxing, as we have steadfastly acknowledged, is an exceptionally dangerous and violent sport. Boxers are not reducible to fictional characters, and the rounds of a boxing match are not a collection of chapters in a novella. A fight plan in boxing is, after all, a plan entailing mutual endangerment; a story about how best to land actual blows on another human being (and avoid succumbing to such blows) through the constrained maximization of constitutively violent skills and the imposition of will. Despite the obvious parallels briefly noted in the previous section, a boxing fight plan is not a 'game' plan in the same sense that one might have for non-violent sports such as tennis or curling, or even dangerous but non-violent sports such as mountain climbing or surfing. For a fight plan—and its various narrative iterations emergent between rounds—is ineluctably about maximizing constrained but creative and constitutively skilled violence in ways that enable an athlete to impose her or his will on an opponent in a manner that inevitably does *physical damage* (long-lasting and often permanent) to that opponent. As Sugar Ray Leonard once said: 'You don't play boxing'.

In sum, in the flow of a professional boxing match, a fight plan contains a unique kind of aesthetic, oriented not toward beauty or truth but the improvisational articulation of a meaningful (if often improbable) narrative of dissimulative (mis)representation to be realized only through constitutively skilled violence. In those 60 seconds between rounds, a boxer and a corner continually confront the need to (re)fashion narratives (fight plans) of overcoming and the skilled imposition of will in pursuit of victory.

At the same time, they share an acute, if unstated, awareness of the violence and danger peculiar to their endeavor. Indeed, in boxing every fight plan must be balanced by the coach's/trainer's ongoing obligation to protect the boxer from the immediate and long-term physically damaging effects inherent in its pursuit. In fact, in a violent combat sport such as professional boxing every second of the time between rounds is (or should be) laden with concern for the physical well-being and existence of the man or woman in the ring. For a professional boxer who has taken too many punches is in a categorically different situation from, for example, a hockey goalkeeper who has surrendered too many goals or a pitcher who has served up back-to-back home runs in the first inning. A coach's decision to keep the latter athletes in the game is not one that is likely to put at risk their physical health or long-term well-being in any real way. Yet as we shall see in the next chapter, in a combat sport such as pro boxing such a moral calculation is an unavoidable part of a coach's ongoing duty to a boxer, not merely as an athletic means to victorious ends but more fundamentally as a person whose ends are quite literally in the corner's hands during the bout.

Notes

1 Nietzsche (1873/1954); translation mine.
2 The focus here is on boxing. But for a discussion of this kind of aesthetic orientation and Nietzsche's account of the aesthetics of existence, see especially Nehamas (1985). And for helpful discussions of Nietzsche and sport more generally, see Tuncel (2016) and Rosenberg (2008).
3 Following Cantor and Hufnagel (2012), we might call such storylines of overcoming '*thumonic* narratives', which are widespread in competitive sport.
4 See Scott (2009), Rotella (2004) and Boddy (2008), for example.
5 Of course the pre-existing framing narratives often affect the fight plans. For example, an up-and-coming young professional is typically expected not merely to win, but to win in a spectacular fashion by knockout, and thus has the incentive to devise a strategy to achieve such a result.
6 Though clearly there are cases—not infrequent—in boxing when an athlete refuses to listen to his or her coach and pursues a narrative or 'fight plan' that only he or she has authored. There are also cases, even more numerous, of boxers concealing injuries (such as a broken hand) from their corners. More obvious, and even more problematically dissimulative, are those cases in which a boxer has a facial fracture (broken orbital bone or jaw bone, for example) that is apparent to all in attendance but is not told so by his cornerman.

References

Boddy, Kasia. 2008. *Boxing: A Cultural History*. London: Reaktion Books.
Cantor, Paul and Paul Hufnagel. 2012. 'The Olympics of the Mind: Philosophy and Athletics in the Ancient Greek Word.' In *The Olympics and Philosophy*, edited by Heather Reid and Michael Austin, 49–67. Louisville: University of Kentucky Press.
Nehamas, Alexander. 1985. *Nietzsche: Life as Literature*. Cambridge, MA: Harvard University Press.

Nietzsche, Friedrich. 1873 [1954]. 'Über Wahrheit und Lüge im außermoralischen Sinn [On Truth and Lie in an Extra-moral Sense].' In *Friedrich Nietzsche: Werke in Drei Bänden*, edited by Karl Schlechta, 309–322. München: Carl Hanser Verlag.

Rosenberg, Melinda. 2008. 'Nietzsche, Competition, and Athletic Ability.' *Sport, Ethics, and Philosophy* 2 (3): 274–284.

Rotella, Carlo. 2004. *Good With Their Hands: Boxers, Bluesmen, and Other Characters from the Rustbelt*. Berkeley: University of California Press.

Scott, David. 2009. *The Art and Aesthetics of Boxing*. Lincoln, NE: University of Nebraska Press.

Tuncel, Yunus. 2016. 'Nietzsche, Sport, and Contemporary Culture.' *Sport, Ethics and Philosophy* 10 (4): 349–363.

10 Cornerman ethics

Arguments about the immorality of boxing, and combat sport in general, are nearly as old as the sport itself, and it is not to our purposes here to rehearse them by way of a closing chapter. Indeed, rather than rehash such debates, I want to close with a consideration of the ethics of *coaching professional boxing*—a topic that has received notably less attention.[1] For while the basic Kantian notion that athletes are to be respected and treated as persons—or inviolable 'ends in themselves'—by their coaches is both commonsensical and well-established, in the case of pro boxing the fulfillment of this kind of coach-specific duty to athletes as persons, while it may come to fruition in sparring, more often than not proves elusive in the heat of competition.[2] To be sure, the referee and the medical doctor assigned to a professional match are required to monitor both boxers' physical condition and prevent a certain degree of harm. But it is the corner/coach who has the *obligation* to the boxer as a person—the others are simply doing their jobs in a contractual-legal sense. In this closing chapter, I want to scrutinize the oft-overlooked complexities and contradictions entailed in fulfilling the cornerman's moral obligation to a boxer in the course of professional competition, where the stakes—ethically, professionally and health-wise—are exceptionally high.

Any discussion of the between round ethics of cornering a boxing match must begin by taking a step back to examine the practice of matchmaking in professional boxing—an issue touched on earlier, but one that merits further elaboration here. For the coach in professional boxing occupies an unsavory role in a sport that is equal parts athletic competition and flesh-peddling trade.[3] Admittedly, in several senses, coaches in boxing, like coaches in many other sports, play a role that far exceeds that of educator and personal trainer; they are also mentors, dieticians, and psychologists. Moreover, in boxing, as in many other sports, coaches typically serve as amateur medics as they tend to their

DOI: 10.4324/9781003196693-10

athletes' injuries in the course of competition. Yet in another sense, and *unlike* in most other sports, boxing coaches are implicated, however indirectly, in the matchmaking process peculiar to the professional version of the sport. That process of matchmaking, with the exception of 'big-name' Las Vegas-style fights where two equally matched boxers are featured, is one in which, in collaboration with a promoter, a coach typically seeks to match a talented boxer (typically younger and with an unblemished but not extensive or prestigious record of wins) against a lesser 'opponent' for the purpose of developing the former's skills, extending her or his unbeaten or near perfect record, and paving the way to a 'big money fight' (a relative phrase in boxing) down the road. In this widely practiced kind of matchmaking both the coach of 'the boxer' and that of 'the opponent' agree to a professional match that is intended by design to be less than fully competitive.

In this way boxing coaches routinely violate what Russell (2018) calls 'duties to foster a context of competition' (82) and engage in a problematic, if seemingly unavoidable, moral compromise that is part and parcel of professional boxing—either encouraging their boxer to take a 'step-up' fight against an established but still lesser opponent or, in the reverse case, pressuring their fighter to 'stand in' as an opponent for a boxer in need of his next 'step-up' fight.[4] If coaching is, as Simon (2013) has argued, a moral practice, then it must be admitted that the position of the coach in professional boxing is morally ambivalent long before the fight ever takes place. Indeed, in light of the matchmaking process peculiar to professional boxing, any suggestion that coaching pro boxing is a straightforwardly moral practice already merits a certain measure of skepticism.

Yet the matter is even more difficult than it may at first glance appear. For this kind of matchmaking, while it transpires outside the ring, generates profound moral questions and dilemmas when it comes to competitions inside the ring. Indeed, in professional pugilism the moral position of the coach vis-à-vis the boxer is especially uneasy, and even conflicted, in the course of competition. All boxing coaches openly express the mantra that they are obligated to be honest about their boxer's progress, physical condition, and probability of success in the course of a bout. Yet the sport of boxing demands that athletes 'go out on their shield'. What this means in practical terms is that in boxing matches athletes surrender their moral autonomy to fight on or quit to their corner: in the course of combat a pro boxer can choose how to fight, but not when to quit.

Consequently, a cornerman accepts, however tacitly, the burden to take on the obligation to treat his boxer as a person and not, say, a fighting machine or an animal.[5] And all competitive boxers genuinely depend on the fulfillment of that obligation in the throes of a match. From their vantage point, it is the explicit duty of the corner—and not the fighter, given the strong taboo in boxing against 'quitting on the stool'—to protect an athlete from too much harm and end the bout by 'throwing in the towel', if necessary.

But despite the best of intentions, for the professional boxing coach gauging what counts as 'too much harm' and realizing such a moral obligation between rounds is elusive. This is not because boxing coaches coarsely treat their fighters as 'things' in the course of competition. The situation between rounds is complex, and often poorly understood by those outside the sport. When a fighter returns to her or his corner, at first glance it would appear that one of three things has just happened: she or he won the round, she or he lost the round, or she or he fought to a draw. That is technically correct insofar as it presents one of three possibilities for how the round has been scored by the judges. But for a boxing coach there is always the fourth possibility—namely, that in winning or losing or drawing the round, the boxer 'took a beating' or 'got beat up'. In other words, the number of blows received threatens not only immediate victory but also the health and future of the athlete—not merely as a competitor but as a person. That is to say that in getting 'beat up' an athlete risks being transformed from boxer (person) to punching bag (thing).

In pro boxing there is a big difference between getting hit (even repeatedly) and getting *beat up*. It is the latter, in the form of numerous devastatingly clean blows to the head, ribs, and liver, for example, that shortens a professional career in the sport and, in time, leads to permanent injuries. And getting beat up does not necessarily mean the fighter was knocked down, or is even necessarily bloodied. On the contrary, some of the most strong willed fighters—those with 'granite chins', as the saying goes—are able to withstand tremendous punishment round after round without going down. In fact it is with those boxers that the cornerman most evidently faces the dilemma identified here: shall he goad his indomitable fighter onward, devising a revised dissimulative narrative or fight plan loaded up with metaphors and metonyms of will, violence, and victory, however improbable and risky? Or, alternatively, is the corner now bound to jettison the fight plan aesthetic and instead act on his obligation to protect the boxer's personal well-being by stopping the fight?

As it happens, the answers to such questions in the context of 60 seconds between rounds are hardly clear-cut, and entail a contradictory and empirically elusive mix of considerations inherent in the work of a professional boxing coach. Indeed, from the standpoint of a cornerman even a short list of such minute-long considerations would at the very least typically include the following:

- his boxer's performance in the previous round (just how poorly did things go?)
- his boxer's overall physical condition (just how bad is she or he, physically?)
- the physical condition of his counterpart in the opposite corner (just how bad is the *other* fighter?)
- stage/round of the fight (getting beat up in the later rounds is the most physically damaging to a career)
- his boxer's previous experience of 'being in tough' (has she or he been in this kind of brutal 'war' before? If so, how did she or he handle it? Has she or he been in too many 'wars'?)
- his boxer's proven durability/ability to take a beating and win (having 'been in tough' before can be an advantage, but 'having been in tough' too many times is not)
- his boxer's demonstrated punching power (having 'heavy hands' is always an advantage in a sport in which an athlete can be completely out-pointed, hopelessly behind, 'out on his feet' (semi-unconscious) and yet win with a single blow—what we earlier called 'the lottery moment' in combat sports)
- his boxer's age, record, and performance in most recent fights

However calculated, achieving balance and properly weighing such considerations is the central moral and professional task of a boxing coach between rounds. For example, a corner's decision to improvise a narrative to fight on may damage a boxer's health and shorten her or his career. But it could also lead to a dramatic upset victory and, more importantly, a bigger fight with a much larger paycheck in the near future; in a sport where remuneration is almost always modest, for both boxer and corner this is no small consideration. Conversely, a corner's decision to end a match may preserve a boxer's personal well-being while at the same time harming her or his athletic chances for a bigger (more lucrative) fight down the road; it may also, perversely, make it possible for an older boxer to prolong her or his career in cases where retirement would be the most prudent and safest option.

Moreover, it must be recalled that the outcomes resultant from a corner's decision-making between rounds in non-marquee fights are themselves embedded in and shaped by the widespread pre-existing narrative of 'the boxer' and 'the opponent' previously discussed. A coach whose athlete is matched as 'the boxer' has much more at stake—professionally and athletically—in winning the fight; indeed, the advancement of her or his career in the sport (and identity as what is known as an 'A-side' or premier fighter) is dependent in no small way on winning the fights she or he is 'supposed to win'. In such cases, a coach's interest in creating successful dissimulating narratives characteristically overrides—or, at the least, fosters a strong incentive to postpone—any duties to protect an athlete's health and personal wellbeing during the fight.

Contrastingly, if ironically, the coach whose fighter is matched as 'the opponent' has more leeway to negotiate the tension between dissimulating narratives and fulfilling duties. The coach of 'the opponent' needs only encourage her or his boxer to go a few rounds and work hard before legitimately 'throwing in the towel' to protect her or his safety and future career, however limited and unlucrative that career may be.

Thus cornering (coaching) in a professional boxing match is informed by contradictory demands of fight plan aesthetics and cornerman ethics. Put another way: coaching a pro boxing match entails both the need to produce dissimulating narratives of will imposition and overcoming, and the obligation to treat a boxer not merely as an athletic means to victorious ends but rather as a person who has yielded her or his own autonomy to surrender in the course of the fight. In fact, in the flow of competition balancing the promise and dangers of the art of dissimulation with the fulfillment of moral obligations to the boxer is the core dilemma of a professional boxing coach. In this regard to coach professional boxing is to engage in what is at best an ambivalent moral endeavor.

To be sure, the period between rounds in boxing finds rough analogs in other sports that contain designated intervals of athletic respite and coaching input—a time out in which to diagram a specific last-minute play in basketball or ice hockey, a half-time inspirational speech in an American or European football locker room, or a manager's visit to the mound to discuss strategy with his pitcher in baseball, for example. All these can and often do make a difference in the outcome of athletic competitions, and may contain contradictory moments of the art of dissimulation and demand of moral obligation as described here.

But the period between rounds in a constitutively skilled violent sport such as boxing crystallizes a unique—and uniquely problematic—set of narrative practices and moral demands. For in pro boxing, athlete and coach engage in a complex set of shifting narratives and obligations structurally similar to but in crucial ways fundamentally unlike what one sees in other competitive but non-combat (that is, not constitutively violent and mutually endangering) sports, where the danger of dissimulation is not so great and the moral autonomy of the athlete is not so attenuated.

In short, a discussion of cornerman ethics—when considered from involvement in the early stages of matchmaking to coaching during the period between rounds of a professional bout—raises what is surely one of the most distinctive and pressing moral questions about coaching pro boxing, namely, the extent to which professional boxing inevitably tends to erode the moral duty sport coaches have to treat their athletes as persons and not things. Of course, most professional boxing coaches care about their athletes as persons (and not just as revenue-generating entities), and ritually admit the need to protect their fighters from 'taking too much punishment' in competition. But the complex dynamics of the sport itself—matchmaking outside the ring and competition within it—do not make such a duty readily realizable. Inevitably, then, it would seem that to coach professional boxing is to engage in a morally fraught endeavor not found in other competitive but non-combat forms of sport. Hence critical accounts of the ethics of boxing would do well to consider not merely the morality of the mere existence of the sport but also the ethical pitfalls entailed in coaching it at the professional level.

Notes

1 For a wide-ranging treatment of the philosophical aspects of coaching, see Hardman and Jones (2011), especially the chapter devoted to ethical issues in coaching dangerous sports. And for a critical discussion of the morality of Olympic youth boxing, see Torres and Parry (2017).
2 On the topic of respect for athletes as persons, see, especially, Tuxill and Wigmore (1998) and Schmid (2013).
3 Wacquant (1988) has explored precisely this point at length.
4 Of course as noted in the foregoing section, the stock distinction between the character of 'the boxer' and that of 'the opponent' is not fixed. The roles can be and sometimes are reversed, as when an 'opponent' scores a convincing upset or as often happens in the later periods of a boxer's career, a boxer's skills diminish over time and he becomes the 'opponent' or 'stepping-stone' for the next generation of successful fighters.
5 Indeed, on a moral level this is arguably part of what makes boxing something more than mere dog-fighting.

References

Hardman, Alun R. and Carwyn Jones. 2011. *The Ethics of Sports Coaching*. New York: Routledge.

Russell, J.S. 2018. 'Broad Internalism and the Moral Foundations of Sport.' *Ethics in Sport*, 3rd Edition, edited by William J. Morgan, 77–92. Champaign, IL: Human Kinetics.

Schmid, Walter. 2013. 'A Kantian Theory of Sport.' *Journal of the Philosophy of Sport* 40 (1): 107–133.

Simon, Robert. 2013. *The Ethics of Coaching Sports: Moral, Social, and Legal Issues*. Boulder, CO: Westview Press.

Torres, Cesar and Jim Parry. 2017. 'Boxing and the Youth Olympic Games.' *Diagoras: International Academic Journal on Olympic Studies* 1: 169–190.

Tuxill, Cei and Sheila Wigmore. 1998. '"Merely Meat"?: Respect for Persons in Sports and Games.' In *Ethics and Sport*, edited by Mike McNamee and Jim Parry, 104–116. New York: Routledge.

Wacquant, Loic. 1988. 'A Fleshpeddler at Work: Power, Pain, and Profit in the Prizefighting Economy.' *Theory and Society* 27 (1): 1–42.

Conclusion

In a critical vein, this brief book has sought to bring together cultural and philosophical analyses of the sport of boxing. Specifically, the study has pursued a culturally informed philosophical critique of professional pugilism. In the most general of terms, the book has advanced its argumentation on three levels.

At the methodological level, I have tried to demonstrate that an adequate understanding of boxing is only to be had if it is viewed as both a cultural practice and a formalized and institutionalized sport. Hence, the study has blended participant and observer, normative and descriptive, and empirical and symbolic approaches to scrutinize professional boxing from the inside out and the outside in, as it were. Put differently, in deploying an interdisciplinary approach to the study of boxing, I have tried to capture some of the many entwined cultural and philosophical aspects of professional boxing in ways that are often omitted in more discipline specific approaches to the sport.

At the cultural level, the first part of the study aimed to make explicit issues of urbanism, identity, violence, socialization, and marginalization at work in the sport of boxing and local boxing gyms. Hence, core conceptions such as pugilistic selfhood, structural violence, boxer cool, and sociation were defined and deployed in an effort to clarify the complex cultural dimensions of the sport.

At the normative level, the second part—informed by the cultural insights gleaned in Part I—endeavored to develop and apply a normative theory of sport robust enough to critique boxing as a culturally embedded but also formalized and institutionalized competitive sport. To that end, I outlined a novel theory of sport—what I called a 'constraint theory of sport'—best able to fuse the cultural and rational features of a combat sport such as boxing, and then went on to use that theory in a critical analysis of pro boxing. In a subsequent series of analyses, the second part of the book sought to develop an account

DOI: 10.4324/9781003196693-102

of combat sport violence, defended the normative potential of sparring in combat sport training, and highlighted the unique—and uniquely problematic—aesthetic and ethical dilemmas inherent in cornering (coaching) a professional boxing match.

In the spirit of critical inquiry, the interdisciplinary positions, conceptualizations, and normative critiques presented here are hardly intended to resolve the many questions raised by a most controversial sport. On the contrary, the modest, but critical, goal of the present inquiry has been to provide a new avenue for thinking about the meaning, value, and, indeed, shortcomings, of a sport that is often poorly understood and badly stereotyped. In other words, this study has not aimed to settle the debates about boxing but rather to provide a new set of perspectives that might inform and further a critical dialog about the *bittersweet* science. That, at any rate, has been the overarching objective of the book.

By way of a speculative conclusion, two final thoughts—one political, the other historical—are in order.

The first: Why is there no union or fighters' association, such as one sees in other violent sports, in pro boxing? Clearly, there is a need for a collective voice in professional boxing. In its absence, professional boxers lack the kind of collective bargaining power possessed by athletes in many other sports. As a result, with the exception, perhaps, of the most notable and highest earning fighters, pro boxers have little to no power over their working conditions, opponent selection, or purse negotiations. At the local and regional levels of the sport, especially, this leads to manipulation and exploitation by managers and trainers/coaches—as we have seen—who often pressure boxers to take fights for which they are not sufficiently prepared or for which they are clearly outmatched. These kinds of imbalanced power dynamics between coaches and boxers carry over into actual competitions as well, as discussed in Chapters 9 and 10, with cornermen often failing to fulfill their moral obligations to boxers as persons during the course of bouts. Unionization would provide professional boxers with the kind of structure and representation needed to pursue assorted workplace grievances, as well as workers' compensation—in particular, disability pay, lump sum benefits, and medical benefits in the case of injury or death. Yet the professional version of the sport is badly fragmented, and, as we saw especially in Chapter 4, boxers themselves seem to lack the kind of broad-based solidarity needed to unionize successfully from within. Moreover, coaches and promoters are in a unique position to frustrate attempts by those outside the sport to unionize it, as they exert profound influence—controlling everything from their athletes' professional progress in the sport to who can enter the gym to train on any given day. Hence, the impromptu appearance of a union organizer or representative in a gym such as Authentic Boxing strikes me as exceptionally improbable.

The second: Whither boxing? As a professional sport, the future of boxing is likely to be increasingly marginal—and not only for the reasons outlined in Chapter 5. The COVID-19 pandemic has, in effect, broken the pipeline of boxers upon which the professional version of the sport depends. Local and regional gyms and competitions have for the most part been shuttered for nearly two years now, and many local urban gyms—already in a precarious state long before the arrival of COVID-19—have closed permanently. For those that have remained open (and Authentic Boxing is one gym that has), training has been severely limited. In practical terms, what this means is that the quality of the next generation of 'boxers' (up and coming fighters) as well as the sheer number of their 'opponents' (those fighters preselected for rising boxers to defeat) will continue to dwindle on the professional scene. Indeed, it is not out of the question to suggest that at the professional level the pandemic may very well force a marginalized sport into a kind of prolonged death spiral—a fate likely to be welcomed by the sport's many paternalistic critics, but one surely to be regretted, above all, by practitioners of the bittersweet science.

Index

Note: Page numbers followed by 'n' indicate notes.

aesthetics: of fight plans 75–77, 79, 86; and pre-existing narratives 76–78, 85; and truth 76, 79; *see also* dissimulation
Albertyn, D. 17n2
Ali, M. 13, 16, 44, 59, 62
amateur boxing 60–63
American Bowling Congress 36
Anderson, E. 28–30
Anderson, W. 24n1
Authentic Boxing Club 8–9, 16, 21, 23, 37–38, 42–43, 46, 91
'the Badlands' 44–46

'basement bowling' 40n6
black social capital 36
Boddy, K. 17n2, 80n4
bowling 33–39; and African-Americans 35–36; participation in 35–39; and segregation 35
boxer cool 27–29, 31–32, 33, 39, 89
'broad internalism' 57n4; as culturally informed 56

Calzaghe, J. 37
Cherland, S. 40n6
citoyen 34
civil society 35
coaching 2, 75, 82–83, 86–87, 90; *see also* cornering
code of the street 28, 31; *see also* Anderson, E.

community 2, 34–37, 39
CompuBox™ 63
constitutive rules 53–56, 58–59, 63–64, 66–70
constitutive skills 55–56, 69; *see also* Torres, C.
constrained diversion 54
constrained maximization 54–55, 59–60, 63, 67, 72, 79
constraint theory of sport 2, 52–56, 58–59, 89; as both descriptive and normative 56
constraints: constitutive 55–56, 61, 64, 68–69; elective 52–53; structural 2, 52–54, 56, 58, 64; suboptimal 60, 62, 64
cornering 75, 82, 86, 90
cornerman ethics 75, 86–87
COVID-19 91
cultural embeddedness 1, 33
culture industry 43; *see also* fitness boxing

Davis, P. 73n1
disrespect 28, 30; *see also* 'dissed'
'dissed' 30
dissimulation 76, 79
Dixon, N. 65n4, 73n3, 73n6
duties: coaches to athletes as persons 82, 87; of coaches to foster contexts of competition 83

Elster, J. 2, 52–54, 59
embeddedness *see* cultural embeddeness
epistemology of cool 27, 30; *see also* boxer cool
ethics *see* cornerman ethics; *see also* Kantian
ethnoracial awareness/ethnoracialization 37

Farmer, P. 21–22
fighting: as means to 'get cool' with others 30–31; social meaning of 28
fitness boxing 2–3, 42, 46
fitnessization of boxing 43
Frazier, J. 44, 59
Foreman, G. 44, 59

Gaffney, P. 40n3
gamesmanship 26
Gatti, A. 77
gentrification 13n5, 46
Geselligkeit see sociation
ghetto 7, 12, 16, 23, 28, 31, 37, 44; as institutional 21–22, 44; as jobless 22, 24n7, 44; the 'new American' 22–24; *see also* 'the hood'; 'the projects'
globalization 22; *see also* neoliberalism
'ground and pound' 70

Heiskanen, B. 17n1
'the hood' 7, 12, 15–16, 19, 22–24, 27–28, 31, 43; as ethnoracialized 22
Hopkins, B. 37

ice hockey 67–69, 86
identity *see* pugilistic selfhood

Jim Crow laws 35
Jiu-Jitsu 69–70
Joe Frazier's Gym 43–46
Jordan, M. 34

Kansas City 7–8, 12, 14, 16, 21, 46
Kantian 82; *see also* duties

Leonard, S. 79
Lewis, L. 59
'lottery moment' 62–63, 85

lusory attitude 56; and combat sport violence 68; vis-à-vis constitutive rules 56; *see also* Suits

marginality/marginalization 46, 89
matchmaking 61, 82–83, 87; as moral compromise 83
Mixed Martial Arts 2, 43, 46, 66, 69–71
MMA *see* Mixed Martial Arts
moral inflationism 34
moral mutualism 71–72
moral obligations *see* duties
Muay Thai 43, 69–70
mutual betterment 39, 67, 71–72
mutual endangerment 66–67, 79

NASCAR 52
The National Bowling Association 36
National Negro Bowling Association *see* The National Bowling Association
neoliberalism 21–23
neoliberalization 43
Nietzsche, F 76; *see also* dissimulation
'no touch fitness experience' 42; *see also* fitness boxing

Oates, .J 17n2
Orr, M. 36

pandemic *see* COVID-19
paternalism/paternalistic 22, 58, 64, 91
Philadelphia 28–29, 43–46
'the projects' 37
pugilistic nonchalance 26–27, 30–31; *see also* boxer cool
pugilistic pedagogy *see* sparring
pugilistic selfhood 17, 19–20, 22–24, 27, 31, 33, 37, 89; as critical response 23; and reflexive agency 20, 23–24; as self-fashioning 24
Putnam, R. 33–36

'rope-a-dope' 62, 64; *see also* stalling
Rotella, C. 17n2, 18n11
Russell, J. 31n1, 64n1, 66–67, 83

serenity 27; *see also* Wiley
Simmel, G. 40n12
Simon, R. 66, 71, 83
sociability *see* sociation
social capital 2, 33–35, 39; as bridging 35–36, 38; production of 34–35, 39; *see also* community
socialization *see* sociation
sociation 38–39; boxing gyms as sites of 38; as cross-cutting 38–39; horizontal versus vertical 38–39
sparring: as co-labor 73; and cooperative ethos 67, 73; normative potential of 90; as pugilistic pedagogy 72; as 'we' endeavor 72
sport violence 67–69, 71; as associative 68–69; and combat sport 67–68, 71–73, 90; as constitutive 68–69, 71; as constitutively skilled 67–69, 71–73, 77, 79
stalling 61–62, 64
status 23–24, 28, 30–31, 37, 51, 66
street code 28–29, 38; boxers as street code adapters 31
Suits, B. 55–56
symbolic capital 30; *see also* status

teamwork 34, 73; *see also* sparring
tennis 54–55, 63

TNBA *see* The National Bowling Association
Tocqueville, A. 34
Torres, C. 73n2
Trimbur, L. 17n2
Tyson, M. 59

unionization 90–91

'vanishing social capital' 35
Vergara, C. 24n6
Verstellungskunst see dissimulation
violence: 'cultures of' 20, 23; physical 20–23, 27–28, 30–31, 33, 38; structural 20–24, 27–28, 31, 33, 37, 58, 67; *see also* sport violence

Wacquant, L. 17n2, 17n3, 24n2, 24n8, 25n9, 87n3
Ward, G. 40n9
Ward, M. 77
West Bottoms 8–9, 46
West, K. 23
Wiley, R. 27
Wilson, W. J. 24n5
Woodward, K. 17n2, 32n2